The Price of Progressive Politics

The Price of Progressive Politics

The Welfare Rights Movement in
an Era of Colorblind Racism

Rose Ernst

NEW YORK UNIVERSITY PRESS

New York and London

NEW YORK UNIVERSITY PRESS
New York and London
www.nyupress.org

Library of Congress Cataloging-in-Publication Data
Ernst, Emily Rose, 1978–
The price of progressive politics : the welfare rights movement in
an era of colorblind racism / Rose Ernst.
p. cm.
Includes bibliographical references and index.
ISBN-13: 978–0–8147–2248–0 (cl : alk. paper)
ISBN-10: 0–8147–2248–2 (cl : alk. paper)
ISBN-13: 978–0–8147–2257–2 (ebook)
ISBN-10: 0–8147–2257–1 (ebook)
1. Welfare rights movement—United States. 2. Welfare recipients—
United States—Public opinion. 3. Public welfare in mass media.
4. Racism—United States. 5. Racism in social services—United States.
I. Title.
HV91.E76   2010
361.6'140973—dc22   2010011996

New York University Press books are printed on acid-free paper,
and their binding materials are chosen for strength and durability.
We strive to use environmentally responsible suppliers and materials
to the greatest extent possible in publishing our books.

Manufactured in the United States of America
10 9 8 7 6 5 4 3 2 1

Contents

Acknowledgments

I cannot begin to thank all those who contributed to the writing of this book. Though I alone remain responsible for its sometimes provocative prose, I will attempt to put my gratitude into words.

Although one might read this book as a pessimistic view of humanity, *all* the activists and communities I met through this work are a testament to the limitless power of care. The deep commitment of these welfare rights activists to social change is remarkable. In addition to sharing often personal and painful experiences with me, they also opened their homes to me; they welcomed me to join in their direct actions, meetings, and family dinners. In particular, I would like to thank the following women: Cynthia, Elaine, and Trina for their hospitality, wisdom, good food, openness, and for introducing me to Appalachia; Gwen, a one-woman welfare rights machine, for introducing me to the political landscape of Houston; the women in Minneapolis who let me join in their direct actions and watch them school state legislators in the world of welfare; and Chinaza, who welcomed me to national organizing in D.C. I owe a particular debt of gratitude to my welfare rights friends in our own organization: Erin, Erica, Jan, Selene, Yolanda, and Zeondra.

I would also like to thank my extraordinarily supportive committee and faculty at the University of Washington. Andrea Simpson is living proof that mentors—in the true sense of the word—do exist in graduate school and beyond. Her commitment to graduate students' and junior scholars' success and growth is astounding. Brilliant, yet grounded, is perhaps the best way to describe her. Andrea's imprint on this project may be seen from start to finish. Her faith in me, as a person and as a scholar, is a gift that has sustained me throughout this process. George Lovell, who graciously became my chair after Andrea's departure, also deserves much of the credit for this project. George's meticulous feedback, support during and after my fieldwork, and willingness to listen to my (many) complaints made completion of this project possible. Naomi Murakawa jumped into this project with enthusiasm and provided critical insights into research design at the prospectus stage and beyond. Michael McCann offered very thoughtful comments and continual support for my fieldwork. Mark Smith's invaluable research-design advice and flexibility allowed me space to think creatively about my fieldwork. Though she was not part of my committee, Dara Strolovitch, at the University of Minnesota, deserves special thanks for her encouragement and helpful advice at multiple points during this project.

My colleagues at Seattle University have also provided support and advice at the manuscript stage of the book. Angelique Davis, a friend as well as a colleague, read portions of the manuscript and was always there to listen. Connie Anthony also provided guidance on navigating the book publishing process. The members of my Postcolonial Justice Faculty Fellow Group—Nalini Iyer, Tayyab Mahmud, Gary Perry, Jeff Staley, and Sharon Suh—all provided valuable advice about the revision of portions of the manuscript. Fellow members of the Seattle University Department of Political Science as well as my colleagues in Women Studies all provided the needed encouragement to finish the book.

Support for my fieldwork was provided by a generous grant from the Harry Bridges Center for Labor Studies. I would also like to thank Bob Duggan for his support through the Martha H. Duggan Fellowship for Caring Labor, which provided financial support to complete the project.

At New York University Press, Ilene Kalish provided the encouragement and support needed to help me complete the manuscript. Aiden Amos also answered my sometimes esoteric questions about the editing process. The anonymous reviewers of my manuscript offered insightful critiques and suggestions, which were enormously valuable in the final draft stage.

I count myself lucky to have had a wonderful graduate-student cohort full of friends who happen to also be colleagues. First, to the "Bond" girls: Umut Aydin, Kristin Bakke, Ceren Belge, and Erica Johnson. They are proof that it is possible to be a poised, fun, and stylish genius. They all supplied advice and critique at all stages of the project. I would also like to thank Graeme Boushey, Christian Breunig, Onnie Grissom, Arda Ibikoglu, Rachel Joiner, Amy Koski, Chris Koski, Tuna Kuyucu, Sebastien Lazardeux, Neil Parekh, and Pam Stumpo. Alex Berger, David Koren, Andy Taubman, and Rachel Rosenman all kept me levelheaded throughout this process.

Most of all, this project is the result of my family's love and continued support. My uncle Mike taught me that care and curiosity can be one and the same. My grandparents taught me the importance of family. Ben, my brother, the funniest and most patient teenager I know, always kept me entertained, and reminded me that the Supreme Court has roundly rejected prior restraint. My dad, who gave me a passion for a just politics, has always encouraged me to do whatever I want and supported me in it. My mom has always been there for me; she even edited some of my most confusing chapters without complaint. Finally, Seva, who fortunately came into my life toward the beginning of this process, always reminded me what was most important.

Introduction

I see this pattern and it took me years to connect the pieces. Working jobs and dealing with child care issues, paying 50% of my check for child care and then havin' to be asked to leave my place because I chose between child care and payin' my full rent. Or feedin' my kids or gettin' diapers and then forced into situations because I chose not to be a punching bag. And so these are systematic choices that have been mapped out and we need to understand that.

—Grace, California

Well, the strengths of the group, is, first of all—it's a bunch of people that are poor people. And some of the people can get strength from other people. And it goes on like that. We're something like a big family and we, and when one go through something, we all have a little input and try to go through it with them—we don't let 'em go through it alone. . . . Togetherness. Yes.

—Shauna, Texas

On a cold November morning, women huddled around a podium came together to speak. Two months after the levees broke and Congress was considering drastic cuts to the already shredded safety net, it was the time to be heard. The purpose of their gathering on the Capitol steps was to call media attention to the deteriorating state of the already tattered safety net. Yet their message alternated between the searing anger, betrayal, and despair of New Orleans and the stilted jargon of budget cuts. The Katrina speeches were not part of the planned script, yet they were the most urgent and meaningful. Those speeches had to be made. Why did some of the women not understand this need? Why did they not understand the connection between Katrina and further welfare cuts? This book is the story of these women and their struggles with one another to make change. It is the story of welfare parent activists—women of color and White[1] women—confronting their common yet divergent experiences in their multiplicity of identities. It is the story of how some of these women understandably wish away the racist specter of the "welfare queen"[2] through the language of colorblindness, and how others learn or are forced to confront this queen head-on. It is, in short, the narrative of a movement grappling with the contradictions and complications of organizing for social change along the multiple axes of race, class, and gender marginalization.

This book examines the dynamics of movements situated at the crossroads of marginalized axes of race, gender, and class. By definition, these movements are confronted with cross-cutting issues and images that "*disproportionately and directly* affect only certain segments of a marginal group."[3] Welfare rights is an exemplar of a movement that must grapple with such issues, embodied in the convergence of marginalized identities in the infamous trope of the welfare queen. Welfare rights activists face an increasingly difficult task: How do they fight public policies based on damaging images of race, class, and gender identities in an era of "colorblind" racism? How do they navigate these intersectional politics in their own movements for change? While it is clear that the welfare rights movement has been unsuccessful in reframing the image of its members, we know little about why and how these strategic decisions were made at the ground level. As welfare continues to be the central public image of poverty programs, and, perhaps the most despised social policy in the United States, exploring the antecedents and current realities of shifting discourses along the lines of race, gender, and class provides insight into how other movements come to terms with frames that target the most vulnerable among them. In essence, this movement is analogous to Guinier and Torres's allegory of the racially marginalized as the "canary in the coal mine": "Their distress is the first sign of a danger that threatens us all.... Others ignore problems that converge around racial minorities at their own peril, for these problems are symptoms warning us that we are all at risk."[4] If *any* social movement is predisposed to attend to the importance of intersecting marginalized identities, it is the welfare rights movement. As it represents both the real and symbolic consequences of at least three intersecting marginalized identities, with race at its core, the inability or unwillingness to engage with these intersectional dynamics has serious implications for more mainstream social movements.

What mechanisms shape the decisions of such social movement organizations (SMOs)[5] to respond to these cross-cutting issue frames that target the most marginalized among them? Inquiry into the political ramifications of how race, gender, and class interact as "intersectional" identities has only recently emerged as a research area in political science.[6] These analyses, along with their critical race feminist legal scholarship precursors,[7] are crucial in laying the groundwork for understanding the practical realities of social movements. But scholars have left empirical questions about how activists struggle with stereotyped portrayals of their movements and movement members largely unexplored. "Intersectionality" describes oppression as more than simply the compound effects of racism and sexism; instead, it locates this oppression as a unique convergence of differing facets of identity along the axes of race, gender, and class. This book examines these empirical questions through the historical and contemporary lens of a movement that represents this convergence. I examine how the overarching politics of colorblind racism, along with race, gender, and class intersectionality—operational *between* and *within* social movements—affect the ability of social movements to address critical issues of welfare politics.

I first examine whether the historical development of discourse by the women's movement about women and work, in terms of race, gender, and class intersectionality, shaped the way contemporary welfare rights activists respond to the cross-cutting issues embodied in welfare politics. Through an explication of the weak alliance of two major social movement organizations in the 1960s and 1970s, I posit that the response of welfare rights groups to the stereotyping of welfare parents stems from the historical realities of race, gender, and class intersections of framing "work," responsibility, and independence of women.

Second, I explore how contemporary realities of colorblind racism and intersectionality influence activists' willingness to engage with issues of race and class embedded at the core of welfare politics. I investigate these dynamics through an analysis of forty-nine in-depth interviews (conducted between 2003 and 2006) with welfare rights activists in eight organizations across the United States. I argue that women-of-color activists, particularly in organizations in which women of color are in positions of power, confront the intersectional implications of the welfare queen and, by extension, the racial ideology of colorblind racism,[8] while White women activists tend to avoid direct discussions of these issues. Instead, these activists deploy colorblindness frames as a way to avoid confronting the realities of racism. When ignored, race, class, and gender intersectionality limits the ability of social movements to address these cross-cutting issues. Given the fundamental insight of critical race theory that racism, sexism, and classism are interlocking systems of oppression, I argue that any movement that seeks to only address one of these forms of marginalization not only risks fracturing the movement, but also undercuts the central goals of the movement itself.

Racial Representations

Over the past fifteen years, the welfare debate and the subsequent elimination of Aid to Families with Dependent Children (AFDC) as a federal entitlement have been thoroughly dissected from the perspective of historical institutional development, race and gender politics, as well as state development and global changes in capitalism.[9] I investigate the particular significance of the welfare queen trope in U.S. politics as a useful shared point of departure for much of this scholarship. While she is not the focus of this book, this characterization does embody the intersectional dilemmas confronted by all movements for social change based on multiple marginalized identities.

Media, Public Opinion, and Race

This book builds on an extensive body of scholarship dedicated to explicating both the existence of the racialized frame of welfare in terms of news media coverage as well as its effect on public opinion. A number of studies in political science have established that media portrayals of poverty, and more specifically welfare, are racialized. In his analysis of news media stories about poverty over a forty-year period, political scientist Martin Gilens finds that coverage became decidedly racialized as African American in the mid-1960s.[10] Despite changes over time, he finds that as "the differences across different subgroups of the poor both attest, it is the 'undeserving poor' who have become most black."[11] Similarly, Clawson and Trice's analysis of newsmagazine photos reveals that "Blacks were especially overrepresented in negative stories on poverty and in those instances when the poor were presented with stereotypical traits."[12] Employing a race and gender intersectional analysis of the welfare reform debates of the mid-1990s, political scientist Ange-Marie Hancock finds that these images were not only racialized, but also gendered in their convergence around the trope of the welfare queen.[13]

The proliferation of these images has had consequences not only for the terms of policy debates over welfare, but also public opinion and racial attitudes in general. Experimental studies, such as political scientists James M. Avery and Mark Peffley's regarding images of welfare parents, found that opinions of this group became more negative among White respondents when presented with photographs of African American parents.[14] Survey analyses suggest that Americans believe most welfare parents are Black.[15] Political scientist Franklin D. Gilliam found in his experimental study of perceptions of the welfare queen that this raced and gendered image had indeed reached the "status of common knowledge" among participants.[16] Not only did the White and Black welfare queen news stories increase anti-Black prejudice among participants, but they also "encourage[d] viewers to perceive welfare as being caused by individual shortcoming, to oppose federal spending on welfare programs, and to prefer that women play traditional gender roles."[17] Gilliam's results are significant not only with regard to the increasing of anti-Black prejudice, but also for the links between this trope and broader perceptions of poverty and gender roles. This web of race, class, and gender perceptions and politics is the central puzzle of this book.

This convergence of stereotypes in the image of the welfare queen is a constitutive part of broader structures of racism and sexism.[18] Hancock connects individual stereotypes, theoretical analyses of the political function of such an image, and broader trends in public policy. She suggests that a more accurate description of the welfare queen image is that of a "public identity"; that is, one that contains both stereotypes and moral judgments. This public identity functions on both a macro- and micro-level in political discourse, which makes attempts at challenging it a daunting task. She explains that the two driving themes of this identity are economic individualism (beliefs about laziness) and fertility (beliefs about hyperfertility) that reside at the intersection of race, class, and gender.[19] This concept of public identity is particularly useful given that it explains the power of such a trope beyond a single stereotype, to the institutional and individual levels of discourse about individualism, work ethic, responsibility, and fertility.

Intersecting Social Movements

The study of intersectionality in terms of race, gender, and class in the welfare rights movement has largely been focused on either the history of the movement,[20] or more general analyses of the current era of welfare politics.[21] Political scientist Sanford F. Schram's work on the dilemma faced by the welfare rights movement, in terms of framing race in their campaigns, reveals the perils of ignoring the racial dimensions of welfare discourse, although he does not explore the connection between this and the actual practices or strategies of the movement.[22] This book focuses on capturing how the realities of intersectionality affect this movement in a contemporary micro-level setting, while also considering how broader discursive trends may have shaped movement responses to the complicated race, gender, and class politics of welfare.

From a social movement perspective, this book re-centers "power" as a central problem of any movement. Scholars have paid increasing attention to the key role of identity in movements,[23] identity construction and framing,[24] as well as intra-movement disputes,[25] but the linkage between identities as markers of privilege and power within movements appears largely absent from this area of research. Kevin M. Carragee and Wim Roefs assert that social movement and communication scholars who study framing have omitted serious considerations of power imbalances between media and social movements, as well as intra-movement constructions of collective action frames.[26] Carragee and Roefs's claim is particularly relevant in the area of identity and framing. Framing theory portrays identity categories as essentially empty vessels; identities are viewed as relatively interchangeable variables. While a level of generalization across identity categories is certainly fruitful in understanding movement dynamics, this generalization risks glossing over real power imbalances within movements that are a result of specific identities imbued with privilege and power.[27] I argue that race, gender, and class are identities that demand a historically contingent and multilevel analysis of power. One of the best ways to explore this complicated politics of welfare, with race at its core, is through the voices of activists themselves.

Framing Colorblindness

Disciplinary boundaries in the social sciences often impinge on coherent definitions of the concepts of "frame" and "framing,"[28] especially between the media and social movement scholarship discussed in the preceding sections. While I delineate the specific parameters of a frame later in this chapter, I rely here on the definition provided by a sociologist of race politics, Eduardo Bonilla-Silva: "[Frames] are rooted in the group-based conditions and experiences of the races and are, at the symbolic level, the representations developed by these groups to explain how the world is or ought to be."[29] Frames are the building blocks of racial ideologies, of which colorblindness is currently dominant in the United States. Colorblindness, as a racial ideology, circumscribes all political discourse about race in the United States, regardless of whether this discourse supports or seeks to challenge the racial status quo. Colorblindness differs from its predecessor, Jim Crow racism, in that it "explains contemporary racial inequality as the outcome of nonracial dynamics."[30] Colorblindness provides the ideological backdrop for this book, as it both reflects and recreates racial hierarchies in the United States, even among those who work for social change.

Activists resort to multiple frames in describing their own and their organization's views of welfare rights organizing. Frequently, these frames feature elements of gender and class politics as they relate to the question of race and welfare. Importantly, the frames used often incorporate intersecting identities based on the categories of race, class, and gender.[31] They differ, however, in critical yet subtle ways. Understanding how these three categories are perceived in welfare rights organizing allows us to move beyond simple unitary, binary, or double conceptualizations of each. It also reflects the lived experiences of these women as well as the complex array of political options open to these organizations. Bonilla-Silva's *Racism Without Racists: Color-Blind Racism and the Persistence of Racial Inequality in the United States* and Ruth Frankenberg's *White Women, Race Matters: The Social Construction of Whiteness* are both exemplary analyses of how frames around race and gender identities are embedded and negotiated by individuals.[32] In this vein, I examine the types of frames used by welfare rights activists in their attempts to construct messages that not only resonate with the media, elites, and the public, but also reflect their daily lives lived in the intersections of marginalized identities. I depart from these two scholars' works by first examining the particular role of frames in constructing political messages for change, as well as the consequences of these frames for communication between and within movements. I also examine the often muddled ways race, class, and gender are talked about by activists for social change—not just ordinary individuals—in a movement based on perhaps the most despised social policy in the United States: welfare.

Theoretical Argument

I employ an intersectional framework to examine the realities of activists struggling with the complexities of colorblindness and welfare politics. This framework—explored at length in chapters 2 and 5—as articulated by critical race feminist legal scholar Kimberlé Williams Crenshaw,[33] emphasizes the unique experiences and concerns that arise from the multiplicative effects[34] of identities along the axes of race, class, and gender. Multiplicative effects describes oppression as more than the additive effects of racism and sexism; instead, it locates this oppression in a unique convergence of differing facets of identity along multiple axes. Crenshaw's conceptualization of *political* intersectionality highlights the problems many women of color face in social movement groups: "Women of color are situated within at least two subordinated groups that frequently pursue conflicting political agendas."[35] While critical race feminist scholars have developed an insightful approach for understanding the dynamics of social movement groups, research on the empirical effects of intersectionality has only recently emerged in political science.

Two works in this emergent field are of particular theoretical importance for this research. The first is Cathy J. Cohen's study of marginalization and cross-cutting issues in the African American community. Cohen terms the process of subdividing *within* a marginalized group "secondary marginalization."[36] Those who fall within this less privileged category are typically the most vulnerable of the marginalized group and are subject to a symbolic "policing"[37] by the group's more privileged members. This policing occurs as the more privileged members attempt to satisfy the norms and practices of dominant society. This secondary marginalization is most often manifest in the response of marginalized groups to issues that cut across multiple marginalized identities. These issues *"disproportionately and directly* affect only certain segments of a marginal group,"" which is most often due to the multiple marginalized identities of this subpopulation.[38] For example, the racialized welfare queen qualifies as a cross-cutting issue in the welfare rights movement: it targets a group marginalized along the lines of race, gender, and class, even though the umbrella "identity" of welfare receipt may be conceptualized as an identity itself.[39]

Political scientist Dara Z. Strolovitch's recent work on the politics and dilemmas of large, single-identity interest groups (which also ostensibly represent a range of subgroups identified in Cohen's book) demonstrates the systematic tendency of such groups to privilege the concerns of their least marginalized subgroups in their policy advocacy agendas.[40] Strolovitch deftly handles the question of strategic motivations of these interest groups,[41] arguing that an intersectional perspective necessitates a deconstruction of a "zero-sum" perspective on their advocacy choices: "The problem is that all of these organizations are traditionally organized around single axes of discrimination and are sectoral in their analyses of social problems. As a result, these organizations fail to recognize that subgroups of their constituents are caught at the crossroad of multiple forms of disadvantage."[42]

These concepts of intersectionality and secondary marginalization provide the framework for the primary argument of this book. I argue that the response to cross-cutting images in the case of the welfare rights movement is rooted in both the intersectional implications of macro-level discourse of women and work, as well as the more micro-level implications of intersectionality for specific organizations. In other words, political intersectionality, as operational between and within social movements, when ignored, limits the ability of social movements to address these critical issues and confront the hegemonic ideology of colorblindness. As my argument attends to both historical macro-level development of discourse along with contemporary micro-level settings of social movement groups, I divide the explication of this into two parts.

First, I inquire whether the initial development of macro-level discourse about women and work in terms of race, class, and gender intersectionality is crucial to understanding the current response of welfare rights groups to cross-cutting issues. Clearly, the initial framing of issues by the welfare rights movement did not occur in a political vacuum. While it is tempting to immediately look to those who were the most immediate adversaries of such a movement, I argue that the impact of an *allied* movement, the women's movement, limited the development of political discourse available to the welfare rights movement. This is an example of the problematic empirical effects of intersectionality within the category of "women's groups." The welfare rights movement's capacity for self-definition might have been curtailed by the process of frame construction by the women's movement, given the interplay of race, gender, and class between and within these two movements. The discursive meaning of the workplace as a site of liberation was at odds with the historical and lived experiences of many African American women in the welfare rights movement.

The construction of the meaning of "work" for women by the women's movement entailed a closure of alternative views of labor by virtue of the privileged positioning of the movement members by race and class. This not only put the welfare rights movement at a disadvantage in advancing alternative discourses about labor, but also helped to shape a public identity of welfare parents as inextricably linked to this conceptualization of women and work. In other words, the development of the women's movement effectively limited the construction of identity in relation to work in the welfare rights movement. This process of self-definition has had a lasting impact, or partially path-dependent relationship, on the allied movement's capability to challenge prevailing discourse about particular issues shared by both movements—such as the relationship between women's "independence" and the capitalist workplace. This discourse—which is shaped, in part, by the intersections of race, gender, and class at the inception of these movements—constrains the contemporary (or imagined) options for responding to cross-cutting issue frames.

Second, this prevailing discursive framework converges with two other mechanisms that influence the responses of contemporary welfare rights activists to the politics of race and welfare: the realities of intersectionality in these organizations in terms of leadership and secondary marginalization. I posit that as group identities help to shape views of the political world,[43] those organizations with women of color in positions of power are more likely to respond to this cross-cutting issue frame, as this frame signals marginalization along the axes of race, class, and gender. Conversely, those groups that are controlled by White women do not directly challenge or engage this cross-cutting issue not only because these women have different intersectional experiences, but also because of the process of secondary marginalization within the movement as a whole. The key point of connection between this argument and the previous discussion of the development of the welfare rights movement is that macro-level discourse constraints are mitigated on the micro-level, in part, by the presence of women of color in leadership positions in individual groups. Given their triple-marginalized identities, I argue that women of color activists will tend to reject the use of frames that obscure the importance of racial cleavages, and thus challenge the politics of colorblind racism.

Intersecting Movements

Bridging the historical development of discourse around women, welfare, work, and subsequent responses to a racialized frame presented a particular challenge for the design of this book. Therefore, I separated these two elements analytically by time period. Below I outline my approach to the initial development of the welfare rights movement and women's movement, and then move to the focus of this book, colorblindness and the contemporary welfare rights movement.

Between Movements

In addressing the problem of initial framing dynamics in the development of macro-level discourse about welfare, I trace the relationship between the second-wave women's movement and the welfare rights movement. In chapter 2 I examine the relationship between women and work in the initial stages of movement development between 1968 and 1977. I selected the National Organization for Women (NOW) and the National Welfare Rights Organization (NWRO) as representative organizations of the women's and welfare rights movements, respectively. These two groups are ideal for comparison purposes as they were founded on the same date in 1966[44] and were also allies, working (to varying degrees) with one another over the course of ten years. As chapter 2 focuses on how NOW framed its claims about work, independence, and welfare, I analyze documentation produced by NOW to reach its membership: its monthly newsletters.[45] Using the eight platform demands of NOW's 1968 "Bill of Rights," I create eight categories of agenda items for a content analysis of newspapers to determine the level of attention to each issue. These categories function as an issue index to NOW's priorities directed toward local chapters and membership. In addition to coding each newsletter for the eight agenda items, I also include subcategories for welfare or AFDC. In addition, I code all newsletters for any reference to race, and also its connection to poverty. Finally, I include a parallel qualitative analysis of frames contained in select newsletter articles on welfare, work, and independence, which represent the range of NOW's responses to these issues.

Within the Movement

After probing the implications of race, class, and gender intersectionality between two movements, the majority of this book is devoted to the implications of such intersectionality within the contemporary welfare rights movement. This movement is particularly well suited for an intersectional analysis as it is a multiracial, low-income, women-led movement. Indeed, given all that these activists sacrifice as a movement of marginalized women, one would expect that they would be the most sensitive to the organizing challenges presented by multiple marginalized identities.[46] Moreover, one would expect that they, perhaps more than any other progressive or radical social movement in the United States, would recognize the imperative to be intentional about confronting the racist or sexist images of their own movement members.

The contemporary welfare rights movement (2006) consists of small, grassroots, low-budget organizations in approximately eighteen U.S. states.[47] Nine of these organizations are in the South, three in the West, five in the Midwest, and five in the Northeast (some states have more than one organization). These groups range from all volunteer to paid staff and comprise a combination of welfare parent/activists, allies, and some professional organizers. These organizations are designed to be welfare parent-led affairs, and all the ones included in this study have statewide advocacy goals.[48] Each organization was selected at the state level rather than by individual organization or metropolitan area. I selected eight geographically diverse organizations to be a part of the study: California, Minnesota, Montana, Tennessee, Texas, Virginia, Washington State, and West Virginia.[49] Five of these organizations are located primarily in urban environments, while three are located in largely rural areas.

While each organization's environment and membership is often markedly different from the others', they share challenges nationally in terms of the racial demographics of the TANF program and the accompanying racial stereotypes. National racial demographics of TANF are changing. Welfare rights groups can no longer make claims nationally about White women composing the majority of the TANF caseload. Organizations in states with primarily White caseloads were previously able to utilize this statistic to dispel myths about welfare. Whites were the largest group of welfare families in the early 1990s, but no longer.[50] It is unsurprising that as states face increasing pressure to lower their caseloads, White women are finding it easier to find employment and leave TANF for a variety of reasons.[51] Despite these trends in national caseload demographics, individual statewide organizations must also contend with how race and inequality shape their state and local political contexts. The perceptions of how race and inequality function at the state level, however, are often quite different. This tension in national coalition building is explored at length in chapter 7. I observe how these individual organizational contexts and perspectives translate to the national level through participant-observation at the 2005 annual conference of the only national umbrella coalition of welfare rights groups in existence at that time.

In addition to the primary data source of interviews discussed below, I also include poverty rates, racial demographics, state-level partisanship factors, and TANF caseload demographics and analyses of internal organizational documentation as contextual factors in exploring the use of particular frames by organization. Finally, I completed a content analysis of several newspapers' attention to race and poverty in the areas where some of these organizations are located. These data provide a broader picture of the political environment in which these groups operate, beyond the words of the activists themselves. As the analytical focus of this book is frames, however, not organizations, I include these data as useful contextual indicators in understanding broad patterns of frame usage by activists between and within organizations.

Studying Colorblindness

Frames, not organizations, are the central focus of this book. I made this analytical choice for two reasons. First, comparing small grassroots organizations, with varying degrees of financial resources, volunteer resources, and membership size is a risky proposition in crafting a coherent study. This is especially true because the organizations I studied ranged an annual budget size from $250 to $337,178. Obtaining comparable documentation across organizations of this size, given their organizational capacities and often radically different leadership structures, is simply impossible. But these data from different organizations are included in the analysis as contextual variables in order to understand specific patterns of frame usage by organization. It is important to note that while I compare organizations in this book, my primary focus is on the *discursive*, or "meaning-making,"[52] elements of movement activity rather than on presenting a comprehensive representation of all elements of movement dynamics. In other words, while I acknowledge that I am unable to claim that these interviews are an exhaustive sample of all activists in the movement, I am more interested in the *discursive patterns* displayed in the movement, which do have concrete effects on internal movement dynamics: "[Discursive politics'] premise is that conceptual changes directly bear on material ones."[53]

Second, and more important, frames, as an analytical tool, are uniquely compatible with the reality of identity and race politics. As described earlier, the definition of a frame utilized in this project is as follows: "Frames are set paths for interpreting information."[54] Frames operate as filters through which individuals "explain racial phenomenon following a predictable route."[55] I diverge from Bonilla-Silva's view that frames necessarily distort the world in favor of the dominant racial ideology;[56] I use "frame" to connote a lens or filter through which dominant racial ideologies and challenges to these ideologies operate.

Frames are the building blocks of racial ideologies; as such, they both reflect and reinforce (or challenge) racial hierarchies. The dominant racial ideology in the contemporary United States is colorblindness. The challenge of studying race in a context of colorblindness is that race is ever present yet rarely discussed in the open. Frames allow for a deconstruction of this avoidance of race, through silences, key phrases, and stories. More specifically, frames serve four purposes in this book. First, they provide insight into how activists think about race, class, and gender in welfare politics. Second, frames, in turn, provide clues about how their organizations *actually behave*. Third, they are devices to understand the way in which social movement members do or do not communicate across organizations. Fourth, as noted above, they both *reflect* and *reinforce* processes of marginalization pervasive in society at large, which have the ability to undermine the movement's social change goals. Most important, however, they measure the evasion of issues of power and its intersection with identity.[57]

Interviews

Frames are the central narrative in this book; semi-structured, in-depth interviews compose the majority of the data collected for these frame analyses. Interviews and frames complement one another, as both are particularly well suited for investigations of race and identity politics.[58] Andrea Y. Simpson explains why extensive interviews offer incomparable insight in her work on racial group identity and politics: "There is . . . suppleness to this method that is useful for uncovering aspects of a phenomenon that may remain hidden because of the necessary constraints imposed by other methods. The trust that can be established between the researcher and subject in an in-person interview is invaluable when encouraging subjects to define issues for themselves."[59] My status as a welfare rights activist also allows for both a shared understanding of the myriad issues confronting welfare parents as well as a familiarity with the often-contentious dynamic of personalities and politics (colloquially known as "drama") in small grassroots organizations. The interviewees themselves include the following five categories: (1) directors, (2) board members, (3) staff, (4) volunteer welfare parents involved with the organization, and (5) volunteer allies[60] involved with the organization. Based on previous experience in interviewing members in Washington State, the most fruitful method for teasing out these sensitive issues around race is to begin with more structured questions about the functioning of the organization, and then allow for more divergence from the questions as we moved toward issues of race internal and external to the group.

Plan of the Book

Chapter 2 provides an overview of the initial development of social movement frames around women, work, and independence. This chapter investigates the intersectional tensions between allied movements. Rather than probe established institutional structures of power, I examine how the "women's movement" in the 1960s may have inadvertently and unintentionally narrowed the strategic choices available to welfare rights activists in the 1990s. While the women's movement and the welfare rights movement were allied initially on the basis of a shared collective identity of gender, the intersectional realities of race and class oppression helped to inhibit any genuine coalition building between the two. The results of this analysis reveal that there was minimal attention to issues of poverty, welfare, and race in the messages relayed to NOW chapter groups, membership, and supporters. Instead, a prioritization of issues such as employment discrimination indicates the importance this group placed on employment as a tool of empowering, or even, perhaps, liberating women. The particular framing of welfare issues, such as economic (in)dependence and child support, revealed a different perspective of welfare priorities than welfare rights activists. I posit that this was a particular perspective born out of the experiences related to the race, gender, and class identities of the majority of NOW's membership. Regardless of intentions, much of this framing served to reinforce boundaries of welfare parents as the "other." Moreover, the focus on employment as a positive, liberating force spoke to the needs and experiences of a particular stratum of women, and was largely foreign to the priorities of the fledgling welfare rights movement.

Chapters 3, 4, and 5 outline the intersecting marginality frames that activists in the contemporary welfare rights movement employ when discussing the politics of race and welfare. Chapter 3 investigates how the dominant racial ideology of colorblindness conforms to particular frames used by welfare rights activists to describe the way in which their organizations grapple with the politics of race and welfare. These types of frames are separated into two broad categories: traditional and "cosmetic" colorblindness. On the surface, these two frames appear quite different: traditional colorblindness avoids discussion of race (and more important, racism), while cosmetic colorblindness engages directly with a description of racial demographics. Ultimately, however, these two categories share the same underlying evasion of power dynamics inherent in any discussion of race, whether it is external or internal to the welfare rights organization. Both frames are overwhelmingly favored by White women activists rather than women of color activists, although there are important class differences between the usage of traditional and cosmetic colorblindness. This division within colorblindness, I argue, foreshadows the transformation of the dominant racial ideology of traditional colorblindness to its new form, embodied in cosmetic colorblindness.

Chapter 4 investigates the implications of activists using intersections of gender and class marginalization still within the framework of colorblindness. I term these frame categories "gendered colorblindness" and "class colorblindness." Like more general expressions of colorblindness, these frames minimize or avoid discussions of race when used to describe the significance of race for welfare politics. But they accomplish this in a somewhat different manner than colorblindness; these frames operate on the basis of a hierarchy of oppression, where either gender or class oppression is of paramount concern. This type of frame is antithetical to an intersectional analysis that views race, class, and gender as interlocking identities and systems of oppression. Thus, in the erasure of race and racism as a critical centerpiece of all welfare politics, they inadvertently support the reigning racial status quo.

In contrast to chapters 3 and 4, chapter 5 explores "race and class consciousness" frames that *challenge* the dominant racial ideology of colorblindness. These frames transform intersectionality from a theoretical approach to a practical organizing and political strategy. Race and class consciousness frames articulate an understanding of welfare politics in which identity is multiplicative and complex. I categorize the subsets of these frames as structural, political, representational, and experiential. Unlike the frames explored in previous chapters, race and class consciousness frames are used most often by women of color activists. These frames are the foundation of a challenge to colorblind racism.

The few White women who do employ these race and class consciousness frames belong to an organization led by both women of color and White women in Minnesota. I probe the dynamics of this group in chapter 6, as well as political and racial-geographic factors in Minnesota that may contribute to this anomaly among organizations. I conclude that organizational structure and racial composition of leadership may influence the use of these types of frames by White women, thus reinforcing not only the shared sense of mission among group members, but also a similar perspective on the interlocking nature of oppression based on race, class, and gender. The broader questions raised by these findings lead to a revisiting of the social movement scholarship of Frances Fox Piven and Richard A. Cloward with regard to movement goals and the definitions of success. I argue for a more expansive view of movement success not only as a way to fully capture the diversity of movement activities and goals, but also in recognition of the interconnectedness of issues of social justice that necessitate an intersectional alternative to the racial ideology of colorblindness.

Chapter 7 examines the translation of the frames outlined in chapters 3, 4, and 5 to national coalition-building processes. National coalitions offer unique organizing opportunities and perils inaccessible at the state and local level. Utilizing formal and informal conversations, email, and participant-observer data from the annual conference of the only umbrella organization of welfare rights organizations in the United States as of 2005, I outline how a collision between colorblindness and race and class consciousness frames both reflected and recreated debilitating cleavages among women of color and White activists at the national level. I argue that these different perspectives need not enervate this coalition; different experiential perspectives are invaluable to the development of a social movement. But when these perspectives reflect the privilege and power of distinct groups along the axes of race, class, and gender within movements (in the case of the welfare rights movement) and between movements (as is the case between the welfare rights movement and second-wave women's movement), they must be acknowledged, openly discussed, and evaluated in terms of impact on the leadership of the movement. If this is not accomplished, the movement will splinter into competing factions and subvert its own goals. Movements premised on multiple marginalized identities that fail to develop consciousness frames that reflect the reality of these intersecting identities ultimately reproduce the very societal dynamics they seek to change.

To Each Her Own

Race and Class in Gendered Coalitions

Maybe it is we poor welfare women who will really liberate
women in this country.
                           —Johnnie Tillmon, former president and
                                   executive director, NWRO

Each successive federal reauthorization of welfare "reform" has
reiterated wage work as a central indicator of individual moral worth of the
poor. The mantra of "work first" exemplifies the heart of this political consensus about welfare. Policymakers have not wrung their hands over the loss
of parenting time for welfare parents in their drive to move these individuals
into low-wage work. The value of motherhood of low-income women has
been denigrated; children have been viewed merely as obstacles to obtaining
employment, not as future citizens. The politics of race, gender, and class are
deeply implicated in this discourse of personal responsibility that envelops
this consensus about welfare.

This chapter explores through a social movement lens one facet of the
root of this consensus among political elites. Rather than investigate established institutional structures of power, or recapitulate the political popular-
ity of conservative discourse about welfare, I focus on the impact of ostensible allies of the welfare rights movement on the trajectory of the welfare
reform politics. Specifically, I explore how the development of the mainstream women's movement[1] in the 1960s may have unintentionally restricted
the strategic[2] choices available to welfare rights activists in the 1990s debate
over welfare reform. I inquire whether the impact of an *allied* movement
(the women's movement) limited the development of framing discourses
available to the welfare rights movement. These movements are selected as
representative of empirical effects of race, gender, and class intersectionality *within* the category of women's movements—that is, coalitions between

women's movements with different membership and goals. I argue that the construction of discourse identifying labor in the workplace as liberating by the mainstream women's movement involved an implicit construction of work that was incompatible with the experiences of many African American women in the welfare rights movement.

This question of the impact of race and class in gendered coalitions is explored through an examination of the relationship between the National Organization for Women and the National Welfare Rights Organization in the 1960s and 1970s. Happily for this analysis, both organizations were founded on the same day in 1966.[3] I investigate the level of attention paid to issues of welfare and poverty, as well as the framing of women's relationship to work and welfare, through an analysis of NOW newsletters published between 1968 and 1977. This quantitative and qualitative analysis reveals that welfare, poverty, and race were relatively low-salience issues for NOW, while employment discrimination garnered the most attention. After I examine NOW's discourse around wage work and the related subject of child support, I suggest that one mechanism underlying this absence of attention to welfare, poverty, and race was the privileged race and class identities of the primary membership of NOW. The lack of a genuine coalition between the two groups reflected not just a lost opportunity for both organizations; I argue that the largely divergent views of the groups on wage work, economic independence, and other related issues created an *intersectional burden* for the welfare rights movement based on its representation of multiple marginalized identities along the lines of race, class, *and* gender. The development of contrasting discourses about work was not merely a parallel process; the unintended consequences of this tenuous alliance without an authentic coalition between the two movements partially enabled the premature demise of the welfare rights movement's alternative conceptions of the meaning of work for women.

Framing Intersectionality

Social movement scholars of "framing" dynamics concentrate on the importance of meaning-making for social movements.[4] The many studies in the area of framing have investigated "counterframing by movement opponents, bystanders, and the media; frame disputes within movements; and the dialectic between frames and events."[5] What remains under-theorized, however, are the dynamics of movement disputes or contestations between social movements that might be potential coalition partners.

Similarly, New Social Movement scholars have turned attention toward the unique dynamics of identity formation in the process of movement development.[6] Joshua Gamson demonstrates how the dilemmas facing LGBT and queer movements reveal how identities may simultaneously develop and maintain movements while also destabilizing them from within.[7] Gamson draws particular attention to how this process of identity building and deconstruction is dynamic and fluid within movements themselves. While scholars of the civil rights movement have noted the gift of this movement's "master frame" to subsequent rights movements,[8] there has been little exploration of how *allied* movements simultaneously affect one another.

While scholars have investigated both the realized and lost potential of coalition building between the welfare rights and women's movement,[9] little is known about the impact of the women's movement's frame-construction process on the ability of the welfare rights movement to either construct their own complementary or alternative frames around issues of women and work. These studies have focused on the relationship between the two primary social movement groups in these movements, NOW and NWRO.[10] The barriers to an alliance were both structural and ideological. Structurally, Guida West notes that while leaders ostensibly encouraged alliances, these coalitions were few and far between at the local level. Expectations of this alliance were also different, as welfare rights groups expected resource support from NOW, which they did not receive.[11] Another division emerged around the fact that in contrast to NOW, the early NWRO was led mostly by male organizers. Ideologically, the two groups "interacted very little, largely because of their divergent views about work, family, and independence."[12] While scholars vary in their explanation of why this alliance failed, and whether the welfare rights movement may be classified as a "feminist" movement, all concur that this coalition was one that never realized its full potential. I turn now to a theoretical framework that explores these intersectional dynamics of race, gender, and class identities in coalition building.

Intersectionality

The central purpose of this chapter is to inquire about impact of race, gender, and class intersectionality on the initial development of political discourse around work, women, and independence in the weak coalition relationship between NOW and NWRO. As discussed in chapter 1, intersectional frameworks view race, class, and gender identities as multiplicative—that is, they are seen as mutually constitutive categories. Therefore, any analysis of sexism, for example, must interrogate how racism and class oppression are implicated in this form of marginalization. I argue that the alliance between NOW and NWRO is an example of the problematic empirical effects of intersectionality *within* the category of "women's groups." As the mainstream women's movement and welfare rights movement shared space temporally and politically, these two movements necessarily had an impact on each other. I suggest that the intersection of race, class, and gender marginalization limited the ability of the welfare rights movement to construct frames that prioritized women's issues in a different light than those of the women's movement. Specifically, the equation of labor in the workplace as a liberating force involved an implicit understanding of work that clashed with the experiences of many African American women in the welfare rights movement. In contrast to middle-class White women, African American women have historically worked both inside and outside the home.[13] Felicia A. Kornbluh's articulation of this problem of the rhetoric of work and welfare is worth quoting at length as it links this issue of the historical realities of the welfare rights movement to its contemporary predicament: "As confusing as it may be for feminists who have considered work a vital source of independence from men, or for leftists who still believe that the wage-earning working class is in an epistemologically unique position to understand and resist the depredations of modern market culture, the rhetoric of work has become a key weapon in opposition to the rights of low-income people in the United States."[14]

This articulation of "work" as a way to break free from dependence on men limited the development of alternative conceptions of the meaning of work by the welfare rights movement. I argue that the first view of work—as freedom from dependence on men—gained traction by virtue of the privileged race and class positions of mainstream women's movement members. This narrow[15] construction of work and independence had a lasting impact on the allied movement's capability to challenge prevailing discourse about particular issues shared by both movements, such as the sexual division of paid and unpaid labor. This prevailing discourse—which is shaped, in part, by the intersections of race, gender, and class at the inception of these movements—constrains the contemporary options for responding to cross-cutting issue frames such as that of the infamous welfare queen trope, which comprises three marginalized identities (race, gender, and class). Thus, I argue, the welfare rights movement experienced an intersectional burden based on its representation of multiple marginalized identities. This burden made it more difficult for the movement to develop politically resonant discourse around the meaning of work for women.

NOW and NWRO

The social movement groups of NOW and NWRO were selected as representative organizations of the women's and welfare rights movements, respectively. While these are just two groups chosen from a range of organizations within these two social movements, they were arguably the most politically influential. Because of its stature and influence, NOW has been the subject of lengthy accounts focused on the women's movement.[16] Similarly, NWRO garnered attention as the national umbrella group for local welfare rights organizations.[17] These two groups represent the primary facilitators of the images created by both movements and are therefore ideal for comparison. Moreover, they shared a focus on the status of women. I end my analysis of newsletters in the mid-1970s, as NWRO collapsed in 1975[18] during the same period of transition of the women's movement to more interest-group-based activity.[19]

The strained relationship between NWRO and NOW has been recounted in works by Guida West and Premilla Nadasen.[20] I provide a brief overview of this relationship as necessary context for the empirical analysis that follows. Though they were formed on the same day in 1966, NWRO and NOW did not recognize each other in a significant way until 1973 (which is supported by the data presented in the newsletter-analysis section). This was partially due to the organizations' different orientations in their emergent stages. According to West, "NWRO emphasized women's traditional role and dependence on men and thus clashed sharply with NOW's thrust for women's economic independence through paid work in the labor market. NWRO's organizers and planners at that time apparently supported the traditional male and female stereotypes, while the feminists were organized to change them. NWRO's justification for its stand was that black poor women's choices were extremely restricted within the economy. Relegated to the lowest-paying and menial jobs, poor black women saw child rearing and a guaranteed income as more attractive and rational alternatives."[21]

By 1972 the leadership of NWRO changed dramatically, though the membership did not. George A. Wiley, the executive director, resigned and Johnnie Tillmon filled his position. Nadasen notes that this transition heralded a shift in the organization: "Black women took complete command of NWRO, both formally and informally."[22] It was at this point that NWRO began to see itself as a part of the women's movement,[23] although its relationship with NOW remained strained. The first time the NOW newsletters mentioned NWRO was after Tillmon became director and the organization experienced financial crisis:

MESSAGE FROM WILMA SCOTT HEIDE—N.O.W. PRESIDENT:

The National Welfare Rights Organization, N.W.R.O., with whom we have worked in coalition and support on many issues, and whose orientation is becoming more feminist, is having serious financial difficulties.

Members of N.O.W. not already members of N.W.R.O. may want to know that there is a support group called "Friends of N.W.R.O."[24]

While NOW's rhetorical recognition of the interconnectedness of women's concerns in this area increased, *action* was scant until the late 1970s: "Toward the end of the 1970s, NOW began to take some action around poor women's needs, seeking to make the feminist organization more inclusive, in accordance with its stated principles."[25] This admission of the lack of action on this and broader related issues—race and class—was highlighted in one of the last NOW newsletter issues included in this research: "Feminists must be outspoken on race and class issues and make a perceivable difference in the lives of minority working class and poor women before we can develop the mass movement that we pay lip service to."[26] As the following sections demonstrate, even a rhetorical recognition of NWRO or poverty in general, at least in terms of communication with membership and local chapters, was quite limited. This fact underscores the tension between these two organizations.

(En)Coding NOW

As this chapter focuses on the question of how NOW framed its claims about work, independence, and welfare to its own members, I analyze documentation produced by NOW to reach its membership. Newsletters to local chapters, membership, and supporters offer an opportunity to view how a group collectively presents itself, as opposed to the relatively contentious discussions often prevailing at board meetings, for example. They also serve a function of "unifying" many diverse local chapters, at least rhetorically. Moreover, specific references to coalition links with NWRO reflect both national and local chapters' action on the issue of welfare rights. Given the critical importance of the formative years of an organization in shaping messages to membership and fostering the strength of coalitions with other groups, I coded the first ten years of newsletters produced by NOW from 1968 to 1977. These sixty-nine newsletters included material regarding both the national organization as well as individual chapters.

NOW's "Bill of Rights, 1968"[27] provides an ideal map of the organization's priorities. These eight goals outline the major issue areas of the organization. As each goal corresponds to concrete policy changes, I created codes based on the eight demands articulated in this document. As article length varied both within the newsletters as well as over time, I coded sentences rather than articles as a better measure of attention. The total number of sentences coded in these sixty-nine newsletters was 32,579, of which 11,367 were devoted specifically to the eight issue areas included below. In coding these sentences, I erred on the side of being overly generous in determining whether a subject could be counted in the area of welfare and poverty, so as to create a generous estimate of attention by NOW to these issues. The eight areas outlined below were coded according to the following broad policy areas: (1) ERA, (2) employment discrimination, (3) maternity leave, (4) child/home-care tax credits, (5) child care, (6) education discrimination, (7) welfare/poverty, and (8) contraception and abortion rights. The demands of the NOW Bill of Rights were as follows:

1. That Congress immediately pass the Equal Rights Amendment to the Constitution;
2. That equal employment opportunity be guaranteed to all men and women;
3. That employers be legally required to provide maternity leave and to allow women to return to their jobs within a reasonable time after childbirth;
4. That the tax laws be revised to provide home-care and child-care tax credits;
5. That publicly funded day care centers be established;
6. That all discrimination in education be prohibited by law;
7. That poor women be given the same access to job training and public housing opportunities as men, without prejudice based on their status as mothers, and that the current welfare system be reformed;
8. And that all laws limiting access to contraception and abortion be removed from current penal codes.[28]

Why create a coding framework based on this document? First, as these demands represent the goals of the organization, they should ideally be reflected in the NOW newsletters, which update members on policy issues and activities. These newsletters also provide an index to determine which issues were given priority. Second, the latter portion of the coding analysis centers on the attention to race in these newsletters.

Determining the intensity of attention to these issues, especially in relation to welfare and poverty, provides a glimpse into whether race and poverty captured any (even rhetorical) attention in the organization. Finally, I include a qualitative examination of some key articles on welfare and work in a later portion of the chapter, in order to obtain deeper understanding of how the issue of work is framed in relation to welfare and notions of (in)dependence.

NOW'S Agenda

The results of the coding analysis reveal that welfare, poverty and race were relatively low-salience issues for NOW from 1968 to 1977. Other demands listed in NOW's Bill of Rights consistently gained more attention than poverty, such as employment discrimination, ERA, and abortion/reproductive rights. These results also confirm the weak coalition between NOW and NWRO. I first explore poverty/welfare attention, race in conjunction with poverty, and then turn to specific issue themes that highlight the results of this analysis.

Attention to Poverty, Welfare, and Race

As noted previously, scholars have noted NOW's rhetorical commitment to issues of poverty in the 1960s and 1970s, but they have also stressed the absence of action on these issues. The results of this newsletter analysis go further to suggest that, over time, there was relatively little rhetorical attention to poverty and welfare in the primary communicative medium connecting the national group, local chapters, and members. Unsurprisingly, NOW newsletters from the ten-year period surveyed prioritized employment discrimination,[29] the ERA, and abortion[30] over issues of poverty. There were demands included in NOW's Bill of Rights that ranked below poverty in terms of attention, but these issues (such as tax credits for child care) were narrowly defined enough that this result is to be expected. As figure 2.1 demonstrates, employment discrimination, the ERA, and abortion received the most attention, while child care tax credits, maternity leave, and abortion/poverty issues ranked among the lowest-attention items.

Discussions of abortion, which initially revealed fissures within NOW (Freeman 1975), consistently appeared in these newsletters. Thirty-eight percent of the sentences that referenced poverty—a broader category than just

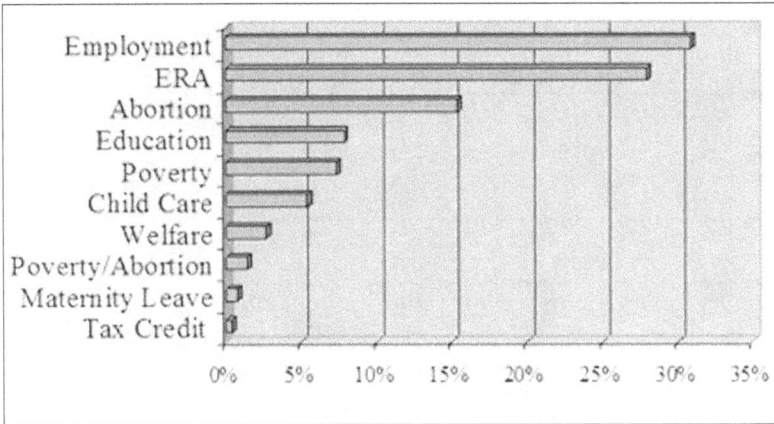

Figure 2.1. Total Issue Sentences, NOW Newsletters, 1968–1977

welfare—were also coded as reproductive issues. This attention to abortion is the flip side, if you will, of the issue of employment explored above. Much like Hancock's identification of the twin themes of the welfare queen trope— lack of work ethic and hyperfertility—the same pattern seems to be reproduced by the NOW newsletters.[31] While the content of these messages may be different, this emphasis on reproduction—even in the few sentences that reference poverty as a whole—belies a similar pattern to the one identified by Hancock.

While figure 2.1 represents a total that is representative of the ten years surveyed, figure 2.2 illustrates the variation in attention to select issues over time. As expected, attention to the ERA, as a proportion of the eight issues included in the coding analysis, intensified over time as NOW devoted itself increasingly to this issue. As achievements in reducing formal employment discrimination were secured, the trend line indicating a lower attention to these issues is also to be expected. Attention to welfare issues remained consistently low, although there was a slight uptick around Nixon's Family Assistance Plan in 1971. We also see an increase toward the end of the 1970s as NOW and other women's groups began to devote slightly more attention to poverty issues after the demise of NWRO.

References to the coalition with NWRO were similarly infrequent: NWRO is mentioned only *eighteen times* over the course of ten years (32,579 sentences total). A similar indicator of the scant attention paid to NWRO is the fact that the organization's first mention did not occur until 1973, six years

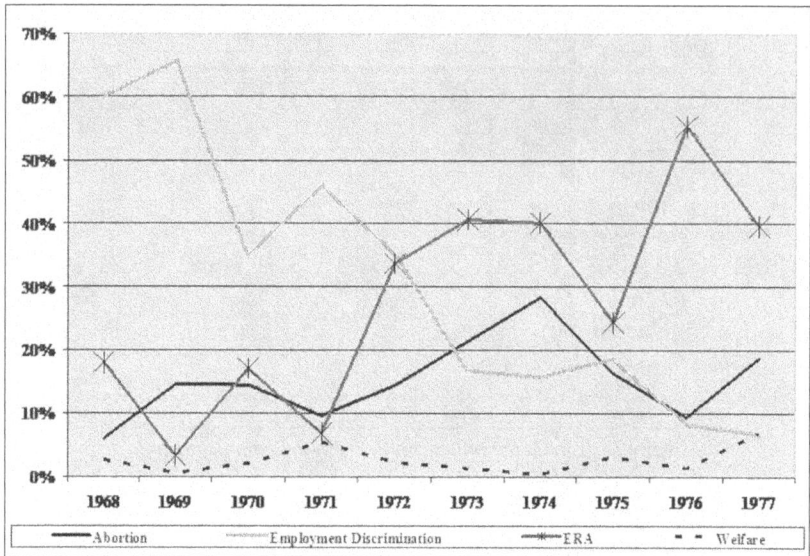

Figure 2.2. Coverage of Issues, NOW Newsletters, 1968–1977

after the start of the newsletters included in this analysis. The "In the NOW News" section of *Do It NOW* newsletters in 1974 includes two examples of the few efforts to advocate on behalf of welfare issues mentioned in NOW newsletters:

> Cincinnati NOW strongly opposed the efforts of an Ohio legislator to require sterilization of all welfare women after their second "out of wedlock child."

> Ohio NOW, through the Right to Choose Fund, is providing the legal expenses for a suit being filed by Ohio ACLU against State Auditor Joseph T. Ferguson, who is withholding payments for approved abortions for state Welfare recipients.[32]

Even here, however, these issues were connected to abortion rather than welfare, a tension further explored below. While attention to issues of welfare was low, evidence of a coalition with NWRO was almost nonexistent. Attention to race throughout all the newsletters is similarly scant. While it is difficult to interpret these results as they represent a minuscule percentage of the total sentences included in the newsletters, it seems that the attention level is relatively low by any measure (figure 2.3). Over the course of the ten-year period of sixty-nine newsletters, race was mentioned in approximately 3% of the total sentences.[33]

Was there an overlap between references to race and to poverty? Approximately 6% of the sentences that mentioned poverty also contained references to race. The newsletters reveal that NOW was concerned, at least rhetorically, about being perceived as a White, middle-class organization. These concerns rarely seemed to translate into any concrete action, however, other than passing resolutions at an annual conference or the occasional involvement of local chapters with welfare rights. A July 1974 report provides a glimpse into the actual demographics of NOW's membership:

- Most ages 20–49
- 91% female
- 36% college grads
- 21% masters degree
- 9% doctorate degree
- 63% worked fulltime outside the home, 22% did not
- 90% White; 5% Black; 3% Mexican/Spanish American, Puerto Rican; 1% Oriental; 1% other
- 81% heterosexual, 8% homosexual, 9% bi, 2% celibate
- Household incomes: 46% $2,500–14,999; 37% $20,000–39,000[34]
- Half were married, with singles forming just over a third of NOW's membership
- 73% were parents, 25% say they did not intend to have children[35]

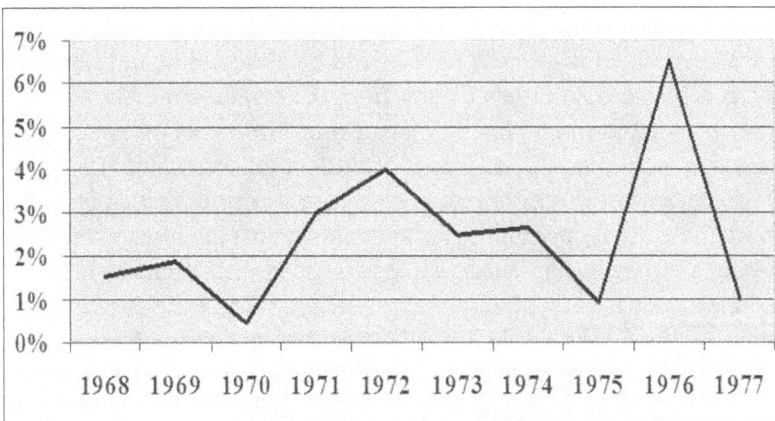

Figure 2.3. Total Sentences Referencing Race, NOW Newsletters, 1968–1977

While the newsletters expressed this anxiety about perceptions of the organization as White and middle class, NOW's attention to White, middle-class issues was a source of frustration to those in the welfare rights movement. NOW received an anonymous letter from a welfare parent that articulated this dissatisfaction: "[You've] done nothing. . . . Your movement is a farce and a travesty to us, because you uphold the forces that make us beg for our existence. . . . Your silence consents to our misery. How dare you call yourselves Sisters."[36] This sentiment expressed not only a frustration with inaction, but also an antipathy toward a group that "upholds the forces that make us beg for our existence." This perspective is perhaps most apparent in NOW's framing of welfare and work.

Welfare and Work

How did NOW newsletters frame this issue in relation to the concept of work in their relatively few references to welfare? Given the dearth of substantive discussions of welfare, particularly in the early years of NOW, it is difficult to draw any specific conclusions about their perspective on this issue. But the types of issues they highlighted under the title of "welfare" (e.g., job training versus a guaranteed income) do provide a glimpse into the way this issue was framed to membership.

A closer examination of the scattered references to welfare indicates that there was little consistency in the way this issue was framed over the ten-year period surveyed. The possible reasons for this are twofold. First, welfare garnered little attention by the organization; this is borne out by secondary accounts as well as the newsletter analysis above. Second, welfare was not an "action" item for NOW. As for the first point, it is reasonable to expect that this, or any other low-priority issue, would be presented in an inconsistent way as it garnered so little attention from the membership. The following question posed to candidates for Congress in 1976 by NOW includes language that is close to the position of NWRO in understanding the value of caregiving as work: "Will you support welfare reform so that all parents in poverty have equal opportunity for job training on a full or part time basis, housing and family allowances, while preserving their rights to remain in the home to care for children if they so desire?"[37] The following year, however, a relatively long article, titled "Housewives and Other Shut-Ins," was devoted to denigrating welfare parents: "The housewife has a handicap, too. She is a dependent, a secondary creature whose identity is based on economic dependency. In our society, economic dependence is a disability. If you are on welfare, you are a dependent on the government. If you are a housewife, you are dependent on a husband. Being economically dependent is like being physically handicapped. You are a cripple, not a fully autonomous individual."[38]

These inconsistencies are explicable precisely because these discussions were abstract, sporadic, and not necessarily connected to the action plan of the organization. Despite the increase in attention to welfare in the latter years of this analysis, especially in terms of devoting conference resolutions to the topic, there was little to no action by NOW in the area of welfare politics. While this is consistent with previous accounts of the tenuous links between NOW and NWRO, there was little attempt to even rhetorically present this issue in a different light to the membership. In other words, at least in the early years of this analysis, there was little effort invested in portraying NOW as active in welfare rights politics. Of the welfare sentences included in the analysis, only 20 out of 363 (5%) described *any* concrete action by the national or local groups, and none before 1971. I now turn to examine more closely the frames of welfare and work through views of economic dependence and the related issue of child support.

Every Woman Better Watch Out: Intersectional Tensions

Perhaps no statement better captures NOW's view of welfare and work than Johnnie Tillmon's famous quote, "Every woman is one man away from welfare."[39] As president and later executive director of NWRO, Tillmon's statement may be viewed as an expression of the underlying vulnerability that women share in terms of social and economic inequalities, while still attending to the way they are manifest based on race and class positions. Ironically, I argue that while Tillmon's statement was used as a call to action (or at least contemplation) to the mainstream women's movement, its use by NOW actually distorted the spirit of her original statement. This misrepresentation emerged from the differing views of welfare, work, and independence of women. Tillmon's "every woman" statement was utilized in NOW newsletters not as a call for empathy and action in coalition with the welfare rights movement, but rather as a veiled threat: "Make a special appeal to housewives who are not members: Remind them that most of us are housewives and many of us only one man away from welfare."[40] This might be rephrased as "don't let this happen to you," thus distancing the "housewife" from the "other" (welfare parent).[41] Similarly, the statement was liberally altered again in a 1973 newsletter article on poverty: "The real empowerment of women augurs more for the elimination of poverty than any so-called welfare reform advanced so far by any political system in any country. Johnny Tillman [*sic*] of the National Welfare Rights Organization is correct: every woman not economically independent or confident of and prepared for her capacity to be so, may be just one man away from 'welfare.'"[42]

The original statement did not include "not economically independent or confident of and prepared for her capacity to be so." The language of economic independence, and indeed, the language of dependence (also occasionally used by NWRO itself), implies that women actually have the *option* of becoming economically independent. This concept of independence individualizes the problem of poverty; further, it suggests that low-income women actually choose[43] to be "economically dependent" in order to feed their families. Again, the above statement emphasizes wage work as the key to "independence," as welfare is framed as the exact opposite: it is what happens to you when you ostensibly lack the confidence to gain independence. Rather than creating an empathetic frame, which I argue was the purpose of Tillmon's original remark, these distortions of her statement were actually used to recreate and reinforce boundaries between groups like NOW and NWRO. Tillmon intimates this in her famous *Ms.* article titled "Welfare Is a Women's Issue":

> The truth is a job doesn't necessarily mean an adequate income. There are some ten million jobs that now pay less than the minimum wage, and if you're a woman, you've got the best chance of getting one. Why would a 45-year-old woman work all day in a laundry ironing shirts at 90-some cents an hour? Because she knows there's some place lower she could be. She could be on welfare. *Society needs women on welfare as "examples" to let every woman, factory workers and housewife workers alike, know what will happen if she lets up, if she's laid off, if she tries to go it alone without a man.* So these ladies stay on their feet or on their knees all their lives instead of asking why they're only getting 90-some cents an hour, instead of daring to fight and complain.[44]

Again, Tillmon cautions against viewing welfare parents as the "other." Welfare rights activists highlighted the vulnerability of women to the exigencies of an oppressive *economic system*, while NOW newsletters focused on women's reliance on men, whether in the form of a spouse or the state. This point cannot be overemphasized: the White, middle-class women in NOW sought to *reform* the existing economic system for the entry of these women into the workforce; the poor women of color in NWRO sought to *change* the economic system itself. Not only did these women conceive of economic independence in different terms, but their relationship to the concept of dependence clashed: White, middle-class women's entrance to the workforce was contingent on other women providing the caring labor they themselves were expected to fulfill as a result of their raced/gendered roles as mother and wife.[45]

Similarly, NOW's emphasis on child support in these newsletters reveals the intersectional tensions between the two social movement organizations. While just two sentences of all the welfare sentences mentioned the concept of a guaranteed minimum income, twenty-nine were devoted to the issue of child support. Emphasizing child support as a critical welfare issue, rather than, perhaps, a guaranteed minimum income, may be viewed as a rather timid reformist approach given NOW's often-expansive goals. While the members of NOW viewed child support as a feminist issue that would equalize a relationship in which men were not contributing economically, they overlooked the subject's race and class dimensions.

First, as African American women often viewed their struggles in the context of a community that includes men,[46] this emphasis on asking White-controlled institutions (the social service bureaucracy) to intervene in their lives and track African American men would probably turn them away from this issue. Similarly, Dorothy E. Roberts notes how intervention on behalf of children is another way for the state to control the behavior of African American mothers.[47] Second, for poor women, and poor African American women in particular, a focus on child support reinforces this racist/sexist stereotype of hyperfertility among welfare mothers. Third, on a practical level, as "women tend to marry men whose economic backgrounds are similar to their own,"[48] providing child support is of a little assistance if the father cannot pay, especially if the state social service agency takes a percentage of whatever child support he does pay. A brief article in a 1970 NOW newsletter, titled "It's Not Pop Who Pays," connects child support to the issue of rising welfare costs:

As taxpayers try to cope with rising living costs, resentment grows against burgeoning Welfare rolls—and, indeed, the rolls are growing. . . . All too often it is the "free-loading" Welfare recipient who bears the brunt of the resentment. . . . The State Child Support Task Force, by the way, has found that much of the upsurge in Welfare is not taking place in the ghettos but rather in the suburbs where the father is able but unwilling to pay. Result: Mother gets a reputation as a "drag on society" because father refuses to pay child support and public officials refuse or neglect to go after him.[49]

Rather than examining the underlying economic circumstances of welfare parents or emphasizing the work they do as caregivers, the article focuses on fathers as the cause of increasing welfare caseloads. NOW's tendency to identify "a man" and "the man" (the state) as one and the same erase the experiences of race and class oppression that circumscribe welfare parents' relationship to the state. It also denies interdependent relationships of family and community that often allowed welfare parents to evade caseworker intrusion and ensure the survival of their families.[50]

Intersectional Burdens

This chapter explored how the politics of race, gender, and class intersectionality *between* allied movements affects the ability of movements to construct frames over time that prove efficacious in reaching movement goals. The women's movement and the welfare rights movement formed a weak coalition initially on the basis of a shared collective identity of gender. But the intersectional realities of race and class oppression helped to inhibit any genuine coalition building between the two organizations.

Analysis of the first decade of messages relayed to NOW chapter groups, membership, and supporters through its newsletters suggest that the organization paid minimal attention to issues of poverty, welfare, and race. Further, the heightened attention to employment discrimination indicates the importance this group placed on employment as a tool of empowering, or even, perhaps, liberating women. The particular framing of welfare issues, such as economic (in)dependence and child support, revealed a different perspective on welfare than that of welfare rights activists themselves. I posit that this particular perspective was born out of the experiences related to the race, gender, and class identities of the majority of NOW's membership. Regardless of intentions, much of this framing served to reinforce boundaries of welfare parents as the "other." Moreover, the focus on employment as a positive, liberating force spoke to the needs and experiences of a particular stratum of women, which were largely foreign to the priorities of the fledgling welfare rights movement.

The weak coalition between NOW and NWRO signified a real loss of potential political power in movement building across race and class lines. Perhaps more important, however, these divergent discourses around work, welfare, and independence had the unintended impact of creating an intersectional burden for the welfare rights movement. While NOW and NWRO shared the marginalized identity of gender in their political organizing,

NWRO also represented marginalized identities along the axes of race and class. This triple intersection of marginalized identities, I argue, made it more difficult to develop alternative conceptions of work and independence for women put forth by the welfare rights movement. The movement that largely represented one singular marginalized identity based on gender was able to proffer a frame that reflected the experiences of some, but certainly not all, women.

What are the implications of these intersectional burdens for contemporary cross-race coalitions? Again, while the political Right is obviously implicated in the architecture of welfare reform, we must interrogate the silences of ostensible welfare rights allies as well. The absence of alternative conceptions of what work means for low-income women, particularly low-income women of color, was certainly evident in the (lack of) debate over the actual purpose of welfare in the 1990s. I posit that the silence over the meaning of work for low-income women was and continues to be the common ground shared among policymakers; both liberals and conservatives held that welfare parents should enter the low-wage workforce. While these policymakers may continue to disagree on the details about how to facilitate this process (such as providing access to child care), they agree that poor women should work. The irony is, of course, that poor women have always worked both inside and outside the home. For them, cleaning toilets, collecting trash, and working at other minimum-wage jobs scarcely seems a liberating proposition. One welfare rights parent-activist I interviewed, Chrystal, captures the predicament of low-income women today: "I already work hard being a full time mom anyways. And then go show up at McDonald's? So people can scream at me and yell at me for $5.15 an hour to come home to kids who are angry with me because I don't spend any time with them, to read them a book, to tuck them in, to say good night to start all over the next day. It's very defeating. And so what's the point?"

Closing Rank

Power and Colorblindness

The real work of marginalization, however, happens systematically through the daily actions of individuals, many of whom
seem to be nice people who are simply doing their jobs and
have no obvious plan to actively participate in the exclusion of
certain groups. Thus we should be clear that intent or malice is
not a necessary condition for marginalization to occur.
—Cathy J. Cohen, *The Boundaries of Blackness*

Race is the primary political cleavage in the welfare rights movement on three related levels. First, as discussed in chapter 1, welfare is a cross-
cutting issue targeting three marginalized identities along the axes of race,
class, and gender. On the level of macro- and micro-level political discourse
about welfare, however, race is the driving force behind this "public identity" of the welfare queen.[1] Second, regardless of the local organizing context
of particular organizations, this racialization of welfare on a national scale[2]
demands that local organizing must be highly attentive to race. The racism
embodied in and reproduced by the trope of the welfare queen signals how
institutional racism structures welfare policy regardless of geographic context. State policy and state context will mitigate this to a certain extent, but
the overall drive to "responsibilize" welfare parents[3] based on this rhetoric is
still pervasive at a national level. For example, the *policy directives* that guide
interactions between a White, female caseworker and a White, female welfare
parent in a rural, predominately White area of the country are still shaped by
the underlying racism and sexism of national welfare politics. This dynamic
is manifest in different ways depending on context, but one cannot ignore
the fact that policy and discourse about race, in particular, influence these
interactions. Third, I posit that given the multiracial identity of the welfare
rights movement itself, this racial fissure is exacerbated by the racial identity

of movement leaders and members when they attempt to build coalitions both at the level of an individual organization as well as at the national level.

This overarching racial discourse about welfare is the focal point of this chapter. The contemporary dominant racial ideology of "colorblindness" inhabits welfare politics in a variety of ways. At first glance, the language of colorblindness appears to offer a counterpoint to the often overtly racialized discourse of welfare politics since the 1960s. It produces the same outcome, however, by minimizing or obfuscating the importance of racism in both the welfare system and social, political, and economic systems more generally. This avoidance of racism as a pressing social change issue also creates rifts within and between welfare rights organizations. The predominantly White tendency to subscribe to a colorblind analysis of welfare politics fuels this potentially debilitating conflict in a movement that represents many of the most symbolically and materially marginalized families in the United States.

Colorblindness as a Racial Ideology

The phenomenon of "colorblind" racism has gained scholarly attention in the past decade as it has become the hegemonic racial ideology in contemporary U.S. politics.[4] This ideology presupposes humanity (translated as normalized Whiteness[5]) as a category that transcends the boundaries of race, thus erasing the realities of the social, political, economic, and cultural consequences of racial hierarchies. Racism is conceptualized in this framework as rare, overt, and an individual behavioral phenomenon. Therefore, institutionalized patterns of racial inequalities are ignored, and racially coded language is viewed as neutral. Colorblindness, as a rhetorical tool, allows individuals to normalize White privilege and institutionalized racism through seemingly nonracial language.

In this chapter, I divide the analysis of colorblindness into two sections. First, I examine patterns of what I term "traditional" colorblindness among activists. This category includes expressions of colorblindness outlined by Bonilla-Silva: abstract liberalism, minimization, naturalization, and cultural racism. These colorblindness frames are easily identifiable and often rely on rhetoric employed in both everyday and political discourse. I find, however, that these frames do not capture the full range of colorblindness expressed by activists in my interviews. Therefore, I develop a new concept termed "cosmetic" colorblindness. Although this type of colorblindness shares the underlying evasion of racism as an institutional and structural force, it is couched in entirely different language. On a superficial level, cosmetic color-blindness appears to be anything but colorblind, as it incorporates an explicit discussion of race. Ultimately, however, it is a discourse that inherently avoids any connection between race and political, economic, or social power. Cosmetic colorblindness is ultimately a paean to cosmetic diversity: these frames include discussion of race in a context devoid of any institutional or structural significance. People of color become statistics: numbers or bodies to be arranged in a way to satisfy critics, grant makers, and the media. More-over, inclusion of people of color becomes a means to an end, a fulfillment of a requirement of diversity rather than as a genuine commitment to racial justice. In a perverse twist of colorblindness language, these frames *explicitly include race as a way of avoiding a discussion of racism.* This adherence to cosmetic diversity precludes productive engagement with questions of power and privilege in the politics internal and external to these organizations. As I discuss further in later sections of this chapter, understanding the differ-ence between traditional and cosmetic frame usage may be tied to the per-sonal experiences of interviewees with the welfare system. White women are the focus of this chapter, as twenty of the twenty-seven White women inter-viewed used either traditional or cosmetic frames. As working-class women are the most racially progressive group among Whites, according to Bonilla-Silva,[6] these activists' responses provide a critically important examination of the challenges facing racially progressive movements.

The use of cosmetic colorblindness frames by White women in pre-dominantly White geographic contexts appears, at first, to be a common-sense response to an all-White environment. I argue that appearances, in this case, are deceiving. Not only do these frames assume Whiteness as an invisible norm and construct a racial fallacy about the politics of welfare, but they also avoid the question of racial justice at the heart of the welfare rights movement. As I discuss later in this chapter, the equation of the size of the population of racially marginalized groups with the magnitude of the problem of racism is a rhetorical red herring. In some predominantly White contexts, women of color are represented in welfare caseloads in *more* dis-proportionate numbers than in states with larger populations of people of color. This means that while racial demographics are undoubtedly critical to understanding local political contexts, these statistics tell organizers little if they are not examined simultaneously with the underlying dynamics of institutional racism in that same locale.

Traditional Colorblindness

As the dominant racial ideology in the United States, traditional color-blindness is an attractive and accessible rhetorical device to employ when faced with uncomfortably direct questions about race politics. Indeed, welfare rights activists are not immune to the ubiquity of this frame. To avoid "priming" interviewees, direct questions about race were not asked until the concluding portion of the interview. As is the case with any sensitive issue that may reveal weaknesses in an organization, responses to questions about race were sometimes confused or hurriedly dismissed. I suspect that the use of a colorblindness frame by some activists was, perhaps, the uncomplicated and "safest" response, as it is part of a cognitive repertoire to which everyone raised or living in the United States has access. Nevertheless, I assert that the use of this frame—depending on the race and class identity of the activist employing it—reveals both the degree to which their organization has integrated an antiracist perspective into their organizing work, as well as the potential for conflict in coalition building between groups in the movement (explored at length in chapter 7). I explore the dimensions of these frames both by racial identity of interview participants and by organization.

Dimensions of Traditional Colorblindness: White Women

Traditional colorblindness frames were overwhelmingly employed by White women activists. Ten White women (out of twenty-seven interviewed) employed these frames, compared to only three women of color (out of eighteen interviewed).[7] As White women possess institutionalized racial privilege, this finding is not unexpected. But the frames explored in this section do complicate Bonilla-Silva's findings about the racial progressiveness of working-class, White women. The dividing line between the use of traditional colorblindness frames and what I term cosmetic colorblindness by White women is previous or current receipt of AFDC or TANF. All the White women who used traditional colorblindness frames had experienced welfare at some point in their lives. This stands in sharp contrast to those White women who used the cosmetic colorblindness frame, about half of whom had never experienced welfare. In addition, there are notable contrasts in frame usage by organizational context. I will explore these tensions following an examination of four traditional color-blindness frames.

Abstract Liberalism

White women activists utilized the most popular frame in Bonilla-Silva's study, "abstract liberalism,"[8] albeit in a different manner than most of Bonilla-Silva's interviewees. This frame incorporates political and economic components of classical liberalism to explain contemporary racial dynamics. Though activists shunned the economic component of this frame, they embraced the political dimension of liberalism. Economic liberalism in this context refers to choice and individualism in an economic sense, while political liberalism emphasizes equal opportunity.[9] If there is one characteristic that all welfare rights activists share—although they may articulate it differently—it is opposition to neoliberal economic policies. Neoliberalism, at least in the abstract, explicitly rejects notions of social or economic collectivities based on interdependence and dependence. It is rooted in concepts of individual choice and individual freedom. Interdependence, however, is explicitly built into the internal logic of the welfare system itself: an individual must have a dependent to qualify for public assistance. This relationship is most often between a mother and a child, so notions of dependence and interdependence are integral to the construction of welfare rights activists' political goals. In a world where low-income women are subject to the whims of individual caseworkers, the criminal justice system, and social service bureaucracies, conceptions of abstract economic individual choice appear to belong in a parallel universe.

While activists reject the economic conception of "choice," they do not reject tenets of political liberalism that incorporate both individualism (the value of individuality) and humanism. Indeed, recognizing welfare parents as unique individuals in a bureaucracy that systematically denies their individuality, dignity, and humanity is an attractive rhetorical strategy. When placed in a colorblindness frame, the concept of universal humanity appears to transcend race while simultaneously denying its importance:

ROSE: How about in this area? [The organization] has done a lot of work on racism. What has been your experience? 'Cause I know they've had different community events.[10]

JANET: See, [her son], he's half mixed too. And they put him down because he's mixed, yeah. But I won't pay no attention to it because I said it was my fault—it wasn't his. *I mean I don't look at Cynthia [African American activist in organization] because she's a different color than I am because when I look at her I look at her just as the same color as me, you know?* That's the way it is and I don't put her down, you know cause she's a different color than I am. *God made her just the same way he made me.* And they say that his hair is made out of wool, so he might be Black too—you never know! [laughs][11] What are you gonna do when you get to heaven and Jesus is![12]

Janet's statement is a classic illustration of traditional colorblindness. First, she claims that it was not her son's "fault" that he is "mixed." Rather than identifying racism (or even racial prejudice) as a problem, the "problem" is his biracial identity. She goes on to describe herself and Cynthia as both human in the eyes of God. She then defuses the tension of talking about race by infusing humor in her last statement.

This abstract liberalism frame is also employed as a distancing mechanism. It is useful to distance oneself from the problem of racism by asserting an individualistic analysis that emphasizes human fallibility. This form of minimization rejects the implications of power inherent in the concept of racism. In a lengthy conversation about race with Breanna, a White activist in Virginia, I asked her about her experiences at the national welfare rights meeting we had both attended: "[The workshop organizer] kept constantly talkin' about White people bein' prejudiced and I looked at it like this— you know, everybody's an individual." This response to my question about an antiracism workshop rejects the notion that racism is inherently tied to White privilege. Then she also distances herself from individual "racists" ("all White people are not racists"). She goes on, however, to complicate this frame by incorporating class, gender, and power:

> 'Cause my favorite sayin' is that America is run by rich, White men. Which leaves out everybody else whether you're a Black woman and White woman or Black man. You know, if you're not a rich, White man, then you're less likely to be in a position of power. So as a structure, yeah, I agree with that, but a lot of people will talk on, you know, "all White people are racist and all White people is rednecks," and, you know. When I said I got him [pointing in the air, indicating her biracial son,] . . . his grandmother wouldn't even let us stay in her house because his mother is White. *So you know, that race issue, that don't, you know—just like you don't expect—other races don't expect you to stereotype them, don't stereotype us with the rich, White guys sittin' over—that are in power.* [laughs]

She rejects the notion that she has the same power as someone with whom she does not share gender or class status. In this sense, this explanation emphasizes the importance of race, gender, and class intersectionality.

Breanna's statement implicates both Bonilla-Silva's findings about working-class, White women's ability to see and understand oppression in a different manner from White men, as well as the underlying colorblindness that White women use to distance themselves from White privilege.

Minimization of Racism

By far the most popular colorblindness frame among welfare rights activists interviewed, minimization of racism assumes race to be an inconsequential social category and racism to be an aberration, not a systemic, pervasive problem. According to Bonilla-Silva, "Although whites and blacks believe discrimination is still a problem, they dispute its salience as a factor explaining blacks' collective standing."[13] In contrast to the other three traditional colorblindness frames, minimization of racism does not necessarily reject the problem of racism itself; rather, it denies it as a ubiquitous phenomenon. In the case of social movement activists, it is a way of diminishing the importance of racism as a political action item. Moreover, it is a relatively "safe" way to employ colorblindness by merely dismissing race as an issue of any import. As board president of the welfare rights organization in Washington State, Clare uses this frame as a strategic tool to deal with the question of race:

ROSE: How does [the organization] deal with the racial side of welfare in the media? Do they?

CLARE: You know, I don't think we deal with the racial side. . . . I think [the organization] tries and strives to be very fair and get into the racial mix. I think we try to *treat everybody equally*, but you know we have a very intense focus on teaching antiracism and training and keeping everybody with a mind-set of, you know, *being equal to all*. So, you know, *I don't see that as a big problem*. And I don't see it as—with media at all—I don't see that their [the organization's] agenda—it's just to teach our staff, our board members—there are issues, things can be offensive, you know. And we need to be aware of different issues for *different people, different disabilities, different colors*, you know.

ROSE: So, you see the focus kind of being more internal rather than dealing with media—not even dealing with it?

CLARE: Exactly. Our agenda is a bit different. But we definitely keep it in thought and we want our, you know, people who are closest to us to not create a problem and have a better understanding and basically that's it.

ROSE: Well, you've kind of already said this, but issues of race, how have they impacted the organization internally?

CLARE: You know, I don't think they have.

ROSE: Just hasn't really been an issue . . .

CLARE: Um, um. [shakes head]

While Clare does recognize the existence of potential problems, she minimizes it in reference to the media. She then asserts that her organization conducts antiracism training for members. This is, in fact, an exaggeration at best.[14] She then minimizes the issue by asserting that it is not a "big problem." The final minimization takes place in merely listing race as one of many issues her organization grapples with among others. She also simply stops the conversation about race from going any further, especially in reference to the internal politics of the organization.

Minimization frames were also used in geographical contexts where poverty was perceived as either bifurcated between Whites and non-Whites, such as Montana, or in predominately White states such as West Virginia. As is the case with all colorblindness frames, Whiteness is normalized and therefore invisible in the context of discussions about race. This is particularly true in the areas where non-Whites are not only marginalized but also "otherized" in the extreme. This process of "otherizing" occurs when racial "problems" are viewed as peripheral to the immediate geographical context; those people of color who *do* live in the area are subject to a heightened visibility due to the fact that racial constructs are fundamentally about ordering physical bodies.[15] Chrystal, an activist with the group in Montana, illustrates this point in her response to my question about race and welfare:

> *I don't think so much that you have a racial problem here.* There's not very many—the Native Americans basically stay on the reservation—there's maybe three Blacks in Helena, and *you know who they are.* . . . I think that [the organization is] pretty open. Well, first of all, Nicole [White staff member] is just open, Jenna [White executive director] is from a completely different state, Jeanine [White staff member] is from Washington, and I'm from Utah, *so it just doesn't bother me.* D'you what I mean? I don't know what the rest, I think that there are a lot of prejudiced peoples so you have a—I know they were trying to pass a bill about teaching Native American history in the school. Making sure the Natives know about it, and it was like there was a resistance to that and I don't understand why because this is Native American territory!

Chrystal first denies that there is any "racial problem" in Montana. A racial "problem" in a colorblindness framework generally refers to the existence of a sizable group of people of color. Again, Whiteness is the assumed norm. Therefore, the few people of color who do exist are either too few to create a "problem"—"three Blacks in Helena"—or are geographically separated from Whites (e.g., Native Americans on reservations). Interestingly, the ability to "know" who the people of color are in this sense is critical to there not being a "problem." Chrystal then conflates geographical diversity with one's racial background. Finally, she shifts the focus of the question away from the organization and the politics of welfare to a focus on the legislature, an entity over which she has very little direct control. Again, my analysis of Chrystal's response is an attempt to uncover how colorblindness functions in this organizational and political environment, not to cast aspersions on a particular individual. Moreover, the use of these frames has implications for dialogues with activists from different racial contexts, as I explore in chapter 7. Here is one final illustration of this type of minimization by a White activist, Carol, in West Virginia:

CAROL: The racial side. The racial—it is a problem here, but it's not as big a problem as it is in other states because we do have a small population of color. I think it's not very high. Our whole state's not real high. Even though like in areas like Charleston it's a very large group but then we have the outside areas that are very, very sparse. Well, it just depends, I mean 'cause we don't, I mean, we don't base anybody on any color or religion or anything like that. So, they come to us, we just help whoever. If there's a problem that arises, and we've never had one, so I'm not sure. You know, we would fight it because you know everything, even the welfare laws are supposed to be non-discriminative, so . . .

ROSE: In theory!

CAROL: We've never really had that problem.

ROSE: Have you guys ever done like just general anti-oppression trainings or anything like that?

CAROL: No. Yeah, we haven't really done a lot of like dismantling racism or anything like that. If we had more money we would do that too.

Again, the minimization of racism frame appears the most "reasonable" of the four colorblindness frames. This is precisely because Carol is not rejecting the idea of antiracism training; it is just not among the top priorities of the organization. As with all colorblindness frames, she also uses an abstract liberalism frame to defuse the situation by mentioning other axes of discrimination in order to divert attention from the focus on race itself.

Naturalization and Cultural Racism

Naturalization and cultural racism frames did not appear in any of the interviews conducted, either among White women or women of color. Naturalization frames describe racial dynamics as "natural occurrences,"[16] thereby eliminating any responsibility for racial inequality. The direct antecedent of both naturalization and cultural racism arguments is a biologically-based rationale for racism of the Jim Crow era. Cultural racism explanations of the contemporary position of people of color attribute their status to perceived "cultural" shortcomings. The first quote below is an example of a naturalization frame, the second is a cultural racism frame (both are excerpted from Bonilla-Silva's fieldwork on racial patterns of interaction and inequality):

> Hmm, I don't really think it's a segregation. I mean, I think people, you know, spend time with people that they are like, not necessarily in color, but you know, their ideas and values and, you know, maybe their class has something to do with what they're used to. But I don't really think it's a segregation. I don't think I would have trouble, you know, approaching someone of a different race or color. I don't think it's a problem. It's just that the people that I do hang out with are just the people that I'm with all the time. They're in my organizations and stuff like that.[17]

> Hmm, I think it's due to lack of education. I think because if they didn't grow up in a household that afforded them the time to go to school and they had to go out and get jobs right away, I think it is just a cycle [that] perpetuates things, you know, I mean, I can't say that blacks can't do it because, obviously, there are many of them [that] have succeeded in getting good jobs and all that.[18]

The cultural racism attributes highlighted above are often connected to the 1960s "culture of poverty" thesis, popularized by Daniel Patrick Moynihan in his 1965 report "The Negro Family: A Case for National Action." These two frames are also the most explicitly "racist" of the four delineated by Bonilla-Silva. These two rely on explicit generalizations about a racial group, while the other two do so in a more oblique manner. Thus these two frames are generally avoided among welfare rights activists as they are viewed as tools of explicit division.

Traditional Colorblindness: Organizational and Geographic Context

White women used traditional colorblindness frames across organizational and geographical contexts. In Montana, Virginia, Washington State, and West Virginia, White women all relied, to varying degrees, on these frames in describing the politics of race and welfare. The only two organizations whose members did not use these frames were located in California and Minnesota. White women in California, however, did rely heavily on a form of colorblindness that I term "cosmetic," discussed in the next section. The women in Minnesota did not utilize either of these forms of colorblindness; surprisingly, they universally rejected colorblindness frames.[19]

Why were the White women activists in Minnesota exceptional in this respect? Racial context and geography offer unsatisfying explanations, as the state does not stand out in any particular way when compared to the other states in this study. In some ways, it resembles Washington State with one major metropolitan area (Minneapolis/St. Paul and Seattle), but it has a significantly higher White population (see table 3.1).

The racial identity of leadership also provides few clues. The organizations in California and Virginia, like Minnesota, do have some women of color in positions of power, but both groups have White women who nonetheless use the language of traditional and cosmetic colorblindness. As I explain in chapter 6, the combination of organizational leadership structure and the composition of leadership in terms of race and class identities offers insight into why a few White women interviewed do not turn to the easily accessible repertoire of traditional colorblindness or to the power-evasive accounting language of cosmetic colorblindness. I turn now to the few women of color who used this frame, and I argue that their racial identity necessitates a different reading of this frame from that of White women.

Traditional Colorblindness and Women of Color

Three of the eighteen women of color activists included in this study referenced colorblindness during the course of their interviews. All of these women used these frames in conjunction with an explicit race consciousness frame, however, explored further in chapter 5. The women of color activists who used these frames were from organizations in which I interviewed only African American women. One of the insights of intersectional theory is that use of colorblindness frames by women of color may have an entirely different

TABLE 3.1. *Race and Poverty by State and TANF Caseload, 2003*

	African-American	American Indian	Asian American	Latina/o	White American
California					
% of Total Poverty Population [a]	9.3	0.9	10.9	51.4	26.2
% of Group in Poverty [b]	20.1	14.6	12.3	19.9	7.8
% of TANF Caseload [c]	21.9	0.6	5.7	50.0	20.5
% of Total Population [d]	6.2	0.8	11.9	34.6	44.8
Minnesota					
% of Total Poverty Population	16.5	2.5	5.8	3.9	67.2
% of Group in Poverty	34.3	22.0	13.0	9.8	6.0
% of TANF Caseload	32.9	9.8	6.6	8.5	41.5
% of Total Population	3.8	1.1	3.5	3.2	87.2
Montana					
% of Total Poverty Population	n/a	17.8	0.7	3.6	74.3
% of Group in Poverty	n/a	40.1	18.2	25.4	11.8
% of TANF Caseload	0.4 [e]	45.5	0.1	2.4	51.4
% of Total Population	n/a	6.4	0.6	2.0	89.1
Tennessee					
% of Total Poverty Population	30.4	0.7	1.3	4.9	61.0
% of Group in Poverty	25.5	36.7	15.0	28.5	10.6
% of TANF Caseload	58.8	0.1	0.1	1.6	39.4
% of Total Population	15.4	0.3	1.2	2.4	78.7
Texas					
% of Total Poverty Population	16.8	0.4	2.3	58.3	21.9
% of Group in Poverty	24.9	14.5	12.1	27.0	7.2
% of TANF Caseload	30.4	0.1	0.5	50.0	18.5
% of Total Population	11.0	0.4	3.1	35.3	49.5
Virginia					
% of Total Poverty Population	35.0	0.7	2.7	7.0	51.7
% of Group in Poverty	16.4	21.9	5.6	11.8	6.7
% of TANF Caseload	66.8	0.3	0.4	3.1	29.3
% of Total Population	19.3	0.3	4.4	5.3	69.3

TABLE 3.1. *Race and Poverty by State and TANF Caseload, 2003 (continued)*

	African-American	American Indian	Asian American	Latina/o	White American
Washington					
% of Total Poverty Population	6.2	2.9	4.4	17.5	65.7
% of Group in Poverty	20.8	26.3	7.5	24.0	9.3
% of TANF Caseload	15.0	5.4	1.9	15.0	58.3
% of Total Population	3.3	1.2	6.4	8.0	77.8
West Virginia					
% of Total Poverty Population	6.9	0.1	0.9	0.9	89.5
% of Group in Poverty	41.7	22.6	31.2	24.6	17.5
% of TANF Caseload	9.7	0.1	0.0	0.2	89.7
% of Total Population	3.1	0.0	0.5	0.7	94.6
United States					
% of Total Poverty Population	23.5	1.5	3.8	23.8	45.9
% of Group in Poverty	24.7	24.5	11.5	21.9	8.6
% of TANF Caseload	38.0	1.5	2.0	24.8	31.8
% of Total Population	11.9	0.7	4.1	13.9	67.8

a. American Community Survey 2003. The estimate totals in this category do not add up to 100% for the following reasons: The category Latina/o may be of any race. The White American category includes those people who identify as "White Alone, Not Hispanic or Latino." The other racial categories are single race categories (e.g. "Asian Alone"), but may include Hispanic or Latina/os. These percentages also exclude the following alternative racial categories on the American Community Survey: "Native Hawaiian and Other Pacific Islander Alone," "Some Other Race Alone," "Two or More Races," "Two Races Including Some Other Race," or "Two Races Excluding Some Other Race, and Three or More Races."

b. American Community Survey 2003. This row represents the percentage of people within each racial category that live in poverty. Therefore, the totals will not add up to 100%.

c. Office of Family Assistance, 2004. Based on active TANF cases by number of families, rather than just adults or just children. Excludes the following categories: "Hawaiian," "Multiracial," and "Unknown."

d. American Community Survey 2003. The totals in this category do not add up to 100% for the following reasons: The category Latina/o may be of any race. The White American category includes those people who identify as "White Alone, Not Hispanic or Latino." The other racial categories are single-race categories (e.g. "Asian Alone"), but may include Hispanic or Latina/os. These percentages also exclude the following alternative racial categories on the ACS: "Native Hawaiian and Other Pacific Islander Alone," "Some Other Race Alone," "Two or More Races," "Two Races Including Some Other Race," or "Two Races Excluding Some Other Race, and Three or More Races."

e. There were 6,619 active TANF family cases total in Montana in 2003. Of this number, there were approximately 247 African American families receiving TANF.

meaning than the articulation of these frames from a position of racial privilege. In addition, racial consciousness generally infused the entirety of my interviews with women of color. In other words, "race" did not appear just in the last portion of the interview when I prompted women to speak about it—it was present throughout our conversation. Moreover, I posit that the actual posing of the question of race provoked a somewhat defensive position by the three women using these frames, but for entirely different reasons than it might in the case of White women. As a White woman interviewer, asking a question about race to a woman of color, usually an African American woman, may have provoked a colorblindness frame as a way of signaling my inclusion in their own organizing work. This contrasts with the underlying current of colorblindness frames used by White women, where it seems to be a strategy to either erase or subsume questions of race and power by using the language of universalism.[20] Desiree, an African American activist in Houston, simultaneously presents a racially conscious and traditional colorblindness frame:

ROSE: How do you think the public sees TANF parents? Like the image?

DESIREE: They portray 'em as, well . . .

ROSE: Don't be nice about it!

DESIREE: Well, I was gonna say 'cause [both laugh] it's really—I was tryin' to find some nice words! *The public see 'em as Black and Hispanic and, you know, the minorities as we're called. It's like, really it's like they the scum of the earth.* You know everybody that gets TANF are—is like they frowned upon, you know.

ROSE: And do you see that image in the media? Or how do you think the media portrays either, like TANF families or poor people in general in this area?

DESIREE: Oh, the media have a field day with it because it's not even nice. [laughs] That's no way nice.

ROSE: How do I ask this one? How do you, my question is, how do you, how does your group deal with the racial side of welfare in the media—but maybe you can just talk about race and welfare in general. Like how it plays out—how you see it playing out in different ways—in your group, in everyday life—that kind of thing.

DESIREE: Well, you know, in our group, we have, we have a couple of Hispanic, you know, members, and I mean really that's it. I mean, we don't have, *we don't try to pull a race card.* I mean we accept our members as interested in joining and want to find out, you know? And try to help. So, I mean it's like, I mean, we wouldn't try to pull going and say well, you did this to her because she's Black, or you did this to her because she's Hispanic or African, Asian, you know? We wouldn't base it upon that. But I mean some instances, the people will do, you know—it would be based upon that 'cause some things you can say and you can tell by people's, you know their voices, about you know, the way they'll word and everything how things are, you know, what a major factor in this. So . . . I mean, you know.

ROSE: Do you hear people talking about experiencing that at the welfare offices—discrimination . . .

DESIREE: I mean, I've experienced that myself, because I was in front of a hearing officer where she, you know, when, we we're goin' up against like about the Texas Health Steps [children's health program]. And she said that the state sent reminders and I told her, no, they didn't, you know? And she said well, they sent reminders of mine—when it's time to take my dog to the vet, you know, so that's comparing children to animals, you know, so? *I mean I don't think she would have said it that way if I had been, you know, a different color,* so, I mean, you know. So, I imagine that a lot of, and some of those workers in the welfare, well, human resources, [laughs] they, they kinda look down on people that gets it, too. That gets TANF and food stamps. But what people fail to realize, the majority of them sitting behind that desk was once where we were. So you have to crawl before you could walk.

Although Desiree does use a colorblindness frame when describing the racial composition of her organization, she is acutely aware of the racism ingrained in the media and welfare system. Her discussion of race and welfare is notable, as well, for its length. She is willing and able to integrate personal experiences with a systemic analysis of race in a way that stays focused on the question and does not meander into issues of religion, class, immigration status, or universal humanity.

Use of traditional colorblindness frames in the case of women of color (and perhaps among White women as well) may be the result of the everyday racial dynamics of the welfare office. Cheryl, a welfare parent in Tennessee, displays racial consciousness, but also describes the fact that the majority of caseworkers are now African American, thus somewhat muddy-ing the appearance of racial hierarchies and racism in the welfare system as a whole:

CHERYL: I think they basically pointing to the Black people, basically. You know? And then as bein' a recipient when I'm down there and there's more Black people than there is White. And that could be just on the day that I'm there. Yeah, but they point it most at the Black people, I think.

ROSE: What do you think at the welfare office? Do you think there's dis-crimination or . . . have you experienced it yourself?

CHERYL: Not really discrimination but it's like some of 'em don't want to work with you because they feel as though they're doing—they're working and you're tryin' to pinch off them? I mean, you know, and I hate that. I just went down the other day and I say, there's one real preppy lady that works there—she's so nice, "Oh, may I help you"—the others are like, "Stand back." I hate those people do me like that! "Do not come past this line!" I hate it. And then you've got the worker that don't call you back. But our workers here they say have very, very heavy loads.

ROSE: Do you—just from your own experience at the offices—are most of the caseworkers, are they White?

CHERYL: *Mostly Black. Long time ago they were White.* But I don't know if it's—I've heard that they have some type of program. And I know a girl that works at DHS (Tennessee Department of Human Services). They started off on AFDC and got in the program and got a job, so a lot of the *younger Black girls are gettin' jobs there as social workers* or maybe they just be sittin' at the desk answerin' phone calls, you know.

Cheryl's experience points to an underlying racial dynamic present in multiracial cities in the United States: those on the front lines as welfare case-workers are often women of color themselves. These experiences, although articulated and interpreted in different ways, were a common thread throughout the interviews I conducted in Houston, Knoxville, and Oakland. While this complicates the picture of racial inequality on the ground, these organizations can provide analyses of racism of the welfare system as a whole that assist in linking everyday experiences with systemic study of the process of marginalization.

Cosmetic Colorblindness

During the course of coding interviews for this project, I was repeatedly confronted by language that did not easily comport to either traditional colorblindness frames or racial consciousness (systematic analyses of oppression). Eleven White women activists and two women of color activists used such language. On the surface, this language appears to be racially conscious in that it does not directly obscure issues of race, as a White woman from Washington State, Julia, demonstrates in her response to my question about race and welfare:

> Hmmm, well, I think in Olympia by showing pictures. . . . I just think because of our population in Olympia which is predominately White I think they try to break it down, one of those myths that it's mostly African American. . . . I think by putting women in front of the camera—oh, I'm sorry, we do do the media training for the parents and so I think that kind of helps a lot of it because when you get somebody like Shemekia [African American woman] who's just very articulate and you know, you put her up there and that just kind of . . . the poor, the uneducated, the African American, I mean to me that puts a lot of the stereotypes of what the media portrays away. So, I think that, we're trying to provide leadership by giving people tools to confront the media. And Claudia [American Indian woman] had an article in the paper and then they did that, was it last year they did that one on four women? So I don't know if we directly confront the racial thing but at least we try to present different experiences. We don't really talk about the immigrants or . . . internally we do . . .

Julia is willing to talk about race, but in a very different manner than those who utilize race and class consciousness frames (explored in chapter 5). First, as a board member, a position of power in this particular organization, she reinforces her distance from members by discussing how they go about "arranging" bodies of color. She describes how they present "articulate" African American women in an effort to break the racist stereotype of the racialized welfare queen. But she assumes that the problem of these racial stereotypes can be addressed by presenting "articulate" women of color, instead of discussing the underlying racism of media coverage. This response may reflect the mind of an organizer, but it lacks any analysis of power; instead, the focus is on manipulating images to placate rather than challenge the media, the public, and policymakers.[21] Further, as experimental research on the power of the welfare queen image demonstrates,[22] this notion that presenting "articulate" African American women to the media and public will somehow lessen their racism is problematic for another reason. Franklin D. Gilliam's experimental study of White and Black women's "welfare queen" images in the media not only found that any news media story featuring either a White or a Black woman (a fictional woman named "Rhonda" in both cases) increased participants' negative perceptions of African Americans, but, counterintuitively, Gilliam also found that "exposure to the white Rhonda produced the biggest increase in anti-black sentiment. That is, watching a story with the white Rhonda increased negative depictions of blacks by 12 percent compared to the black Rhonda and by 23 percent over the story without a picture."[23] In addition, Gilliam found this interesting wrinkle in terms of gender: "Depictions of white welfare queens also seem to induce whites who describe themselves as having liberal views about gender roles to arrive at extremely harsh views of African-Americans."[24] Gilliam's findings underscore the hopelessness of strategies that rely on the ordering bodies to present to the media rather than attacks on the underlying assumptions about race, gender, and class embodied in media and political narratives about welfare.

Another White board member from the same organization, Helen, advances this language of accounting of bodies a step further:

> Well, I feel like I don't know 'cause I can't think of a lot of examples except that [two women of color mentioned by Julia above] story and I think that does represent a success in doing that—*in choosing people, in choosing people that were both people of color who were on welfare, but were also off welfare and getting off welfare and coming from different backgrounds.* And telling—Claudia [American Indian woman] I think sort of talks about an abusive relationship and Shemekia [African American woman] I'm pretty sure talks about working. So, I think that they, you know, without appearing to have this be a lesson in kind of race image stuff they have . . . obviously it sort of participated in, and entered into the choice. That's the only, I don't think they were the only ones in that story—those were the two I remember. *So, I think it sort of comes out in sort of the savvy in identifying people.* But there's no question that [the organization has] probably got larger minority participation than the welfare caseload as a whole in this state. It's a pretty White caseload. And there is *this tension—you don't want to have this caseload appear only minority when it's not. So it's not clear that it's, that it would be, or is a good idea to have every welfare recipient ever quoted to be a person of color. And it's not.*

Perhaps the most striking feature of this excerpt is the distancing mechanism implicit in the way Helen responds to the question posed. This distance is implicit in the relationship between women activists within the organization (ostensibly led by welfare parents) as well as in absence of attention to *racism*, not *race*. When pressed to discuss these internal issues further, she cannot articulate any concrete action in this regard:

ROSE: Do you know if there's ever been any discussions about that, at like board meetings or anywhere else that you've had?

HELEN: About the media strategy, specifically?

ROSE: Yeah, in terms of like you said, if there's a caseload, there's tension and then all the stereotypes that go along with welfare.

HELEN: Well, there's certainly been a lot of discussion about anti-oppression work at board meetings at retreats and there's been various pieces of it. At membership meetings—you were there. You know, my sense is that there has been, but I can't think of specific instances. I think it's more—it's sort of incorporated in how you sort of evolve—like who would be a good person to talk to the press or who would be a good person to speak at rallies.

ROSE: And the anti-oppression work sort of touches on how does race impact [the organization] internally as an organization? Like the anti-oppression stuff—have there been other things?

HELEN: Well, you know, I think of just, other things about, discussion about media. I think there have been, but I don't think I was there for them, let's put it that way.

ROSE: But even beyond the media, but [the organization] itself as an organization?

HELEN: Yeah, no, there's been discussions in terms of, well, where should we put resources—should we be opening an office in Yakima if we're talking about where are minorities and welfare. And are we a state-wide organization or are we city-based? And who do we serve— race enters into all of those discussions.

Julia and Helen's responses represent the broad outline of cosmetic color-blindness: discussions of race as a method of implicitly avoiding discussions of racism. I now turn to the distinct subcategories of this frame and the characteristics it shares with traditional colorblindness.

Whiteness and the Status Quo

The first characteristic that cosmetic colorblindness shares with traditional colorblindness is the overarching presence of Whiteness as the invisible status quo. According to one Montana activist, for example, "The racial issue is mainly Native American [here]." In this type of frame, people of color are an additive element, wholly separate from the "norm." This is implicit in the "we" used by Pat and Joan, both White activists in Washington State (separate interviews):

PAT: We've been trying to *reach out to different ethnic communities.* Unfortunately, Olympia is not all that diverse as it likes to claim to be. And also language barriers—most minorities in this area do speak Spanish or Korean or something else, so, we had a Spanish-speaking intern which was really, really good, and we could do some outreach but then it's like when she leaves we don't have somebody with like the language skills to pick up where she left off, and so the language barriers have been our, one of our biggest issues in dealing with different ethnic communities. *But it's something that we've tried to figure out ways to bring more people, inclusion, into our group into our organization and see what the needs are of all women but, unfortunately, I wish Olympia was a little bit more diverse.*

ROSE: How have issues of race impacted [the organization] internally? Have they?

JOAN: Well, I think issues of race impact us all the time. I don't know the way, I mean, you know, I'm sure that the Seattle office with its longer history and much more diverse community has a lot more stories to tell on that end. Here, in Olympia, I can't think of any things offhand . . . that we've been internally affected by race. I think it's wonderful that we're doing anti-oppression work because I think that they educate our staff and our volunteers and our board and our members, and hopefully create a more even more welcoming place for women of all races. You know, and one thing I worry about in Olympia is that we are mostly White. The town is mostly white. But I don't want to have an organization that somebody— that a woman of color—doesn't feel like she belongs. So, so, I think about that and try to work with that every day.

Pat's response reconstructs a particular (White) community in which "reaching out to different ethnic communities" assumes a monolithic standpoint of Whiteness. The way in which "ethnic communities" are described suggests they exist on the periphery of the community, both rhetorically and in reality. Joan makes much the same point in her description of their community. Diversity, in this sense, only exists when people of color—a category that overlaps with language groups in the response—are present. Thus Whiteness is rearticulated as the norm, devoid of any racial content. This frame shares the "invisibility" characteristic with traditional colorblindness, but it diverges in the willingness to discuss race, albeit in a context of non-articulated Whiteness.

Management and Neutralization

The second and third subcategories of this frame, management and neutralization, are wholly distinct from traditional colorblindness. These unique characteristics center on the fetishized accounting of bodies, rather than a focus on varied group perspectives and experiences. This is a strategy of implicit avoidance of controversy within the organization, rather viewing controversy as a potential source of organizational growth. Specifically, this frame articulates a vision of women of color as constituting a group of bodies that must be both managed and neutralized if they do not conform to the messages the group wishes to produce.

Management refers to the organization of bodies in a particular space. Elements of class and positions of power (within the organization) emerge as particularly critical in management frames. The activist who uses this frame automatically removes herself from the picture and presents a bird's-eye view of the situation. The quotes from Julia and Helen in the previous section accomplish this when they speak of how their group negotiates with the media. In these descriptions, women of color become bodies that need to be groomed, trained, and presented to the media in order to break a particular stereotype (see also chapter 4). But this presentation treats women of color as somehow separate, different beings that need to be managed and brought out at the "appropriate" moment. This is a privileged dilemma that White or multiracial organizations face. Women of color organizations do not have the option of deciding when and if they will present women of color to members, the media, the public, or policymakers. As they are all women of color, their choices are either to embrace their identities and navigate the treacherous terrain of media stereotypes, or to eschew a public presence entirely. Unless women of color organizations chose to avoid public visibility altogether, they must necessarily contend with the stereotype of the welfare queen.[25]

Neutralization frames are more racialized than management frames. Management of bodies may apply to both women of color and White women who are either relatively new to the organization or in powerless positions. Neutralization, on the other hand, refers to the reduction of race to a trivial cultural trait. This neutralization is embodied in the denigration of the term "diversity" itself in popular culture. Contemporary antiracist organizers eschew "diversity training" as devoid of analyses of power or structural dynamics: "[It] sees racism primarily as the result of individual action."[26] Race, in this context, becomes simply additive, superficial, and decorative. This neutralization is expressed in two specific ways: aesthetically and instrumentally. The first refers to a superficial, "benign" diminishment or avoidance of racism through a discussion of racial demographics; the second includes an accounting of the bodies of women of color as a testament to the legitimacy of the welfare rights organization. In both cases, a surface adherence to racial diversity is paramount while racial justice as an organizational principle is ignored.

Aesthetic and Instrumental Neutralization

Aesthetic neutralization is the most intuitive application of diversity terms: an activist responds to a question about race by asserting the "nice diversity" of the organization. Zöe, a White staff member from Washington State, explains as much in response to a question about the internal racial dynamics of her organization:

ROSE: Do you think race has impacted [the organization] internally at all? In sort of either, what you see in the staff, or what you see in terms of membership, or retaining people or staff?

ZÖE: *I know we have got a nice diversity.* When I first started there was Sue with an Asian descent and June [an African American board member] whose been in here frequently. Since then, Sue has left, but Sally's [an African American member] been coming through—she's Black. Shemekia's [an African American member] still active, I've had two volunteers over the summer. One was a young girl, she'd just turned sixteen—got her through the Seattle Youth Employment Training Program. Great help, fantastic help.

When she first started she'd show up early even for the time she was supposed to be here. Which is incredible for someone of her age, I thought. Because my own daughter isn't that good. . . . You know, I truly appreciate it to have that kind of help, answering the phones, doing some database entry for me, things like that. They help. But she was in a car accident towards the end of the term so she hasn't been in. . . . She's had some health problems—she was absent for like three days out of the summer. But she called before and said, "I'm not coming in today, can't come in." They she told me why and I go: "oh my God!"—she'd just gotten out of the hospital—she'd had a problem with her blood sugar over the weekend or something. But she was conscientious about it—can't come in. The day she had the accident she had somebody else call in—"she had an accident, she won't be coming in"—"OK, is she all right? Don't worry, it's OK!" So, we have a *nice, diverse group—different ages, we get different backgrounds*. We have an elder, not elderly, she's what we call a senior volunteer, a program through Seattle. She's working on a new database project with me. So, yeah, she's originally from New York, she's also named Sue. Makes it easy to remember her name. She's got a legal background—all these neat ideas too. Oh, it would be nice to work with her on some other things.

Instead of describing the implications of race and racism for the internal dynamics of the organization, Zöe relies on a list of women of color in the organization to respond to the question posed. She also minimizes race by using the term "nice" and emphasizing other, less explosive issues of age and "background." Further, she equates race with age, as if it were simply one personality trait among many. This is, perhaps, the most benign expression of neutralization. Instrumental neutralization, however, is more insidious in terms of internal organization dynamics, external relationships between organizations, and relationships with funders. Instrumental neutralization refers to the concern over the accounting of racialized bodies as proof of the organization's legitimacy (linked to grant support) rather than an authentic concern for racial justice. Specifically, White women in positions of organizational power were concerned with the appearance of racial diversity rather than interrogating the meaning of racial justice, even in a homogenous White environment. An assumption that "race" is a synonym for "people of color" underlies this concern about racial demographics rather than racial justice. Funders of these organizations are, perhaps, the most responsible for this problematic approach to welfare organizing—and social justice movements in general. Many White women activists in this study perceived racial diversity to be a necessary box that must be "checked" on a grant application rather than as a baseline principle of their organization. This concern was expressed in the two predominantly White organizations (which came from the states with the highest relative White populations as well). Denise, an activist responsible for grant writing in her organization in West Virginia, uses this frame in her response to my question about race and welfare:

> Well, what we've had, we've had to, not that we've had to, but we've looked at it a lot. Because you know funders want us to have . . . a lot of funders, they want the racial breakdown and stuff like that of our board, members, and things like that so we've become more aware of things like that. *'Cause at first, we didn't really think about that, we were just people that were workin' on stuff.* [laughs] And then as we started thinkin' more about it and [the organization is] *predominately White, but it's not because we all sat around and said, "Oh, we only want White people."* It's because only 3% of West Virginia's minority. So, now, our board, we have, one woman who's on it who's African American. Linda did pass herself as African American sometimes. Linda is White but she had a Black husband and her children are mixed and she lived in the community. And, so, she identifies herself that way sometimes. We have members of color of all different, you know, colors. Like we have a Spanish community that's building up here so we're gonna start reaching out to them some cause we noticed there's this community developing. *And, but, that's an issue that we had to really look at because some people have come in and basically accused us of not having enough racial diversity. And we're like, not for lack of trying!* [laughs] *We're not saying you can't come!*

Denise expresses frustration and insecurity with funders' racial diversity parameters for the organization. This is a real concern for predominately White organizations operating in White environments. Rather than questioning why so few people of color are a part of the organization, however, racial environment emerges as an excuse for the absence. Further, in this framing, race is conceived as cosmetic rather than a substantive issue that is integral to all welfare rights political organizing. Viewing the racism solely in terms of racial demographics in a particular locale is problematic. For example, the American Indian population of Montana is 6.4%, but they compose 45.5% of the state TANF population. In contrast, Texas's African American population is 11.0%, while they compose 30.4% of the state TANF population. This means that the racial imbalance in terms of welfare is *seven times* for the American Indian population in Montana while it is nearly *three times* for the African American population in Texas. These figures suggest that a focus on racism is more imperative, in terms of the relative size of the White population, in Montana than in Texas. The equation of the size of the population of racially marginalized groups with the magnitude of the problem of racism is a rhetorical red herring. Racial dynamics do change depending on size and geographic location, but these facts alone do not reveal the social, economic, or political status of people of color in that area. Racial demographics are useful in examining the dynamics of racism only if the underlying power relationships are interrogated with equal rigor.

In a general sense, the language of cosmetic colorblindness also provides justifications for the absence of a racial-justice component of an organization. Consider the following example: if the population of color in a particular state is small in comparison to other states (in relative terms), this becomes a justification for not integrating antiracist policies and practices into the organization's operating structure. This tendency presents a twofold difficulty for the success of welfare rights organizing. First, it alienates organizations in other states that do prioritize racial justice in their organizations (see chapter 7). Second, it often ignores the underlying racialized perception of poverty even in their own *White* states. This second problem was apparent when I asked Denise (a White organizer) about the perception of welfare parents in West Virginia, which has the highest relative White population of any state in this study):

ROSE: Do you think the image of who is on welfare is racially specific in West Virginia?

DENISE: *I think it's specifically Black* because except for people who we've been able to let them know otherwise and stuff. But the general public, I think it is, they're seeing it as, like I said, *a Black woman who's a crackhead prostitute poppin' out kids, you know.* And it's not because our average—[the West Virginia Department of Health and Human Resources] did a study—the average woman is thirty-two, she's White, she has two children, and she stays on welfare for two and a half years. That's the average. But that's not what they see. *And they still have that welfare Cadillac thing, welfare queen kind of, some people still have that image.*

ROSE: I'm so interested by that 'cause it's just, I would have thought that in Appalachia of all places, the stereotype would have been specifically White.

DENISE: It's not. In West Virginia too, I think it's part of the culture. We have a lot of people who won't accept assistance because they don't believe in getting stuff from the state. And I think that kind of feeds into that stereotype because people, a lot of people have this stereotype that people who are of color are lazy and they're lookin' for a handout kind of thing. And I think that's why it feeds into it even [though] there are more poor White people here. And I think that's what it is.

Denise's picture of the perception of welfare parents in West Virginia, if correct, suggests that race *does* matter in West Virginia, even if Whiteness is the norm. Moreover, if parents in West Virginia are declining public assistance they desperately need as a way of psychologically distancing themselves from low-income women of color, this would seem to be a pressing issue for any welfare rights organization. While this group has attempted to attend to the descriptive racial demographics of their organization, it was not integrated in terms of systematic internal attention to antiracist policies and practices.[27]

On the whole, I argue that cosmetic colorblindness has emerged from the increasing professionalization of the welfare rights movement since the 1960s. The language of cosmetic diversity avoids controversy, conflict, or radical change, and ultimately obscures issues of power both within organizations and in the welfare system more generally. As dominant racial ideologies reinforce and reflect the racial status quo, I argue that this use of cosmetic colorblindness among White welfare rights activists reflects the large-scale emergence of a new racial ideology in the United States.

The Future: Traditional or Cosmetic Colorblindness?

At the opening of this chapter, I explicated established parameters of traditional colorblindness and its role in the contemporary welfare rights movement. In the conclusion to this chapter, I argue that like all racial ideologies, traditional colorblindness will eventually yield to a newly emergent racial ideology. This developing ideology is cosmetic colorblindness, a discourse that will become more pervasive and damaging to the cause of racial justice, particularly in the welfare rights movement.

The articulation of the difference between traditional and cosmetic color-blindness in this chapter adds a layer of complexity to Bonilla-Silva's findings about the racial progressiveness of White women, particularly working-class White women. The overwhelming majority of White women who favored the language of traditional colorblindness in this study had experienced the welfare system at some point in their lives. But the welfare background of the White women who used cosmetic colorblindness frames was varied. I argue that this pattern portends the future of colorblindness as a racial ideology, particularly the ascendant nature of cosmetic colorblindness.

Cosmetic colorblindness is arguably more pernicious than traditional colorblindness. The mask of cosmetic colorblindness, on the surface, appears in much the same light as race and class consciousness (chapter 5): a challenge to the racial status quo. Further, this discourse is not shy in describing racial demographic realities. But it diverges with race and class consciousness in that it obfuscates, marginalizes, and ignores the importance of power in organizational relationships and politics generally. Race becomes a cosmetic trait that must be "dealt with" rather than integrated as a focal point of social justice struggles. In other words, this cosmetic colorblindness frame includes an explication of race, but not *racism*.

Traditional colorblindness is easily deconstructed in antiracism trainings on the institutionalized nature of oppression. But cosmetic colorblindness is the colorblindness of the formally educated and the "sophisticated." Most of the women who use these frames are well versed in the language of racially progressive politics. They often use this language, however, to the benefit of their organization, without applying these principles to the politics of those same organizations. Cosmetic colorblindness is ultimately the racial ideology of those in control in progressive political movements. This emergence of cosmetic colorblindness is the next stage in the development of colorblindness as a racial ideology. Clichés like "some of my best friends are Black" are rapidly becoming the unacceptable language of the past, just as the explicit language of "Blacks as inferior" became (racially) passé with the unraveling of Jim Crow in the 1960s. As suggested above, this discourse is more difficult to challenge, since it has co-opted the language of race consciousness while including the power evasiveness inherent in traditional colorblindness. Finally, as I discuss in the following chapter, these frames garner more strength by their coupling with discussions of the hierarchy of gender and class marginalization, which serve to obfuscate the centrality of racism in the politics of welfare.

Pulling Rank

Gender and Class Colorblindness

With welfare, gender is primary since it is women who are taking care of kids.

—Eve

We don't [play] the race card. When we go to Austin to talk and we speak . . . it's not the race card—it's the rich against poor.

—Gwen

The complex nature of marginalization in the United States demands a more extensive explanation of the relationship between colorblindness and axes of politically meaningful identities.[1] Welfare rights activists' narratives bear out this complexity, particularly in the area of gender and class. Racial ideologies such as colorblindness cannot exist in an identity vacuum; that is, they must attend to the experiential differences in ordinary people's daily lives. Colorblindness must be a flexible-enough discursive lens so that both an unemployed, White man in rural North Dakota and a White, female corporate executive in New York can share an ideological framework that explains the racial order they experience in their daily lives. Racial ideologies such as colorblindness must not only be adaptable in order to remain relevant, as Bonilla-Silva suggests, but must also retain the ability for individuals with different identities to reinterpret them within the basic confines of the original framework.

These interpretations of colorblindness through a lens of gender and class are not merely a by-product of the colorblindness framework; rather, they reproduce it in a meaningful way for the individual deploying such a frame. In contrast to the frames explored in chapter 5, these gendered colorblindness and class colorblindness frames are inherently anti-intersectional; they rank forms of oppression without expressing the way those identities and forms of marginalization interact with one another. In this ranking of particular identities or forms of marginalization based on gender or class over race, race becomes a merely incidental, unimportant, and invisible category, much in the way that race is "erased" by the colorblindness frames explored in chapter 3.

This chapter explores the implications of both gender and class marginalization within the framework of colorblindness. "Gendered colorblindness" and "class colorblindness" describe general frame categories in which activists describe either gender or class oppression as the overriding concern in welfare rights organizing and welfare politics. Similar to the frames explored in chapter 3, White women use these frames rather than those of race and class consciousness (chapter 5). Colorblindness still operates as the overarching structure of these categories; the frames are an active response to the question of race's importance in welfare politics. Therefore, they are either explicit or implicit attempts to minimize the importance of race in welfare rights organizing and welfare politics. Categories of gender and class, in this context, are used as "escape hatches" for Whites to avoid discussing race and racism. While I argue that both frames are problematic from an intersectional perspective, class colorblindness may be more insidious for organizers, as the term "class" is often used to describe a shared income status, not a shared class status. For example, TANF parents in the movement often do not share the same class background, so their perspectives on the welfare system may be markedly different. For example, a college-educated woman who temporarily receives welfare due to a divorce has different expectations of the system than a woman with less than a high school education who uses welfare as a safety net between low-wage, temporary jobs. Therefore, class colorblindness may not only minimize the role of racism in the welfare system but also obscure real differences in class position of movement members.

Gendered Colorblindness

Welfare is, without a doubt, a women's "problem." Social welfare programs crafted during the New Deal, including Aid to Dependent Children (later AFDC), were structured around a two-tiered system based on gender. Programs such as Unemployment Insurance were created on the model of a male breadwinner (and were more generous), while programs such as ADC were premised on a female-headed household that was in need of moral "uplift" (and were less generous). Women and men of color, if they were able to access these types of programs, were most likely to qualify for the less-generous category of programs.[2]

The contemporary demographic realities of welfare participation and rates of poverty clearly indicate the gendered nature of this problem. As of 2001, women made up 90% of the adult TANF population.[3] The welfare rights movement reflects this pattern: it is overwhelmingly composed of and led by women who have experienced welfare and poverty. While few, if any, welfare rights activists would deny the gendered nature of poverty or of organizing, this shared gender identity has become paramount in the minds of some activists. It is this primacy of gender identity that motivates the first of the intersecting marginality frames that are critical to understanding the predicament of the contemporary movement.

"Gendered colorblindness" may be superficially viewed as a response or challenge to the dominant racial ideology of colorblindness. Upon deeper analysis, however, this frame falls into the trap of erasing the critical importance of race in the struggle for welfare rights by privileging an apparently racially "neutral" gender identity, which implicitly privileges White women. Sociologist Ruth Frankenberg's groundbreaking work on the intersection of gender and race in the construction of White women's identities guides much of this analysis. In her study of how White women talk through race, Whiteness and gender were most often "co-constructed" in discussions of interracial relationships.[4] Despite the varied life histories of the women interviewed, Frankenberg created three categories identifying the ways in which these women "made sense" of race: essentialist racism (biological inferiority), colorblindness/power evasiveness (rejection of difference and obfuscation of realities of racial hierarchies), and race cognizance (recognition of difference and relationship to social structures).

The notion of gendered colorblindness put forth in this book both extends and complicates Frankenberg's work in two respects. First, I interrogate how women who would have most probably been marked as racially "progressive" (race cognizant) in Frankenberg's study navigate a hierarchical or intersectional approach to race, gender, and class identities. Similarly, I explicitly focus on those on the front lines of a social movement, not everyday people. Therefore, the frames that women deploy in this context not only have bearing for understanding broader trends in ways people negotiate and think about identity, but also have real consequences for movement mobilization and strategy.

Frame Articulation

In contrast to the traditional or cosmetic colorblindness frames, gendered colorblindness centers on an explicit gender identity and implicit racial identity in describing the problem of the racialization of welfare. I coded these frames by searching for references to "women", "gender," or "sex(ism)" in the responses to my questions about race and welfare.[5] Responses were coded further as gendered colorblindness if the importance of race diminished in relation to the primacy of shared gender status. The following excerpt illustrates this importance of a shared gender identity: "We're just trying to help women in general. Because it does affect women of every race, every background." This activist's response (explored further below) to my question about race and welfare asserts the central importance of a shared gender identity within the context of her organization. Race is minimized as simply a part of one's "background," and thus not as important as shared gender identity. All these gendered colorblindness frames share this trait: they implicitly (or sometimes explicitly) rank sexism as more important than racism in the context of problems facing their membership or in the prioritization of action items by the movement. Rather than constructing race and gender identities as mutually constitutive, they are viewed as separate, discrete entities. I argue that for women of color who explicitly reject a gendered colorblindness analysis, gender/sexism simply becomes a metaphor for Whiteness in the organization. While White women who use this frame may view it as a tool of unification in their organization, I argue that this erasure of difference between women becomes a method of excluding the voices and experiences of women of color. In the sections that follow, I explore the use of these frames and how they vary by (1) racial identity of organizers, (2) organization, and (3) geographical context.

Gendered Colorblindness: White Women

On the whole, this frame was invoked relatively rarely compared to other frames explored in this book. What *is* notable about this discourse is that only four respondents used it to explain their approach to dealing with race, and they were all White. Moreover, all the women deploying this frame were located in Washington State. I will now explore two components of these frames in more detail.

We're All Sisters

The first and most common expression of the gendered colorblindness frame is structured around the notion that all women, despite their "differences," share an essential, nearly identical experience. That is, this frame is premised on an essentialized core of womanhood that ostensibly transcends any differences along lines of class, race, or sexuality. Here are three statements that exemplify this frame by White activists in Washington State in response to my question about how the organization grapples with race, welfare, and the media:

PAT: But it's something that we've tried to figure out, ways to bring more people, inclusion, into our group, into our organization, and see what the *needs are of all women* but, unfortunately, I wish Olympia was a little bit more diverse.

ZÖE: We're just trying to help *women in general. Because it does affect women of every race, every background.* They [women] think they're wealthy and never get touched by poverty.

JOAN: So, we really try to, you know, we constantly, we try to, you know, of course if there is a woman of color who has a story she wants to tell, of course that's great. *Because that's affecting women of all ethnicities and ages,* and, you know. But we try to show that in how we portray things in the media. You know, we try to show that this is happening to married couples, single moms, you know, all across the board and, and we also know that discrimination happens everywhere and it doesn't not happen in the welfare office.

These frames may be interpreted in two ways. First, they "erase" race as an important facet of the general marginalization of women. They do this by simultaneously minimizing race by explicitly "ranking" gender as a shared identity. The notion that poverty affects "all women" implicitly assumes that women all share similar experiences of poverty, which, at least in terms of race, is false. A second, more subtle view of this frame is the "double oppression" model. Theories of double oppression view racism and sexism as compound yet ultimately separate issues.[6] The critique of this theoretical approach by critical race feminist theorists is that it assumes an essentialized "woman" or "person of color," which obscures how marginalized identities intersect to produce wholly different political and life experiences. A simplified view of this is the separation of people of color and women into discrete categories. These frames, however, diverge in one important respect from a double oppression model. Double oppression theories assume racism and sexism as equally important in understanding processes and structures of marginalization. But the frames explored here both implicitly and explicitly place gender oppression at the top of a hierarchy of oppression over other forms of marginalization, including those based on race, ethnicity, class, sexuality, or ability.

Women as Bodies

The second subset of the gendered colorblindness frame includes an additional element of hierarchy beyond ranking gender marginalization "over" race marginalization. This added element is the hierarchical view of organizing held by women in positions of power in the organization. From the perspective of an organizer, this view includes women as strategic bodies to be mobilized to achieve political goals.[7] I include an extended discussion of one White woman's exploration of race and welfare, as her responses most clearly capture this tension in gendered colorblindness:

> EVE: We try to be up front and bust it. That's where it's important to *train women of color to be articulate spokespeople* so that.... It's this real balance challenge of wanting, not wanting to feed into the stereotypes, so.... I have to weigh what, who we're putting up as spokespeople: that divorced women are much more sympathetic than unmarried parents, regardless of race. Women who have a work history are much more sympathetic than women who don't, regardless of race. Women who are doing something, i.e., they're in school or working, or not doing something just by taking care of their kids, which in my mind is as important. You know, so it's this balance—so it really depends on who the reporter is or what the event is—of my kind of sifting through stuff.
>
> ROSE: When you're deciding who it should be ...
>
> EVE: Yeah, yeah. And I'm not even sure that it's conscious, when I go through the card file in my head, but those are all things that play out and I look at.

The "organizer" in Eve is evident in her statement. Members are viewed as strategic tools to be utilized in relaying a message to the media.[8] The notion that organizers must "train" women of color to be "articulate" is indicative of a hierarchical approach to organizing, and one that seems particularly troubling in reference to the treatment of women of color in this organization. The remainder of her statement reinforces the first gendered colorblindness frame discussed: "we're all women." When asked directly about the role of race in the internal workings of the organization, she acknowledges White privilege, but then expects an African American woman, Sally, to take leadership on the issue by herself:

ROSE: How have issues of race impacted [the organization] internally?

EVE: In different ways. White Anglo women, regardless of class, don't always see their skin color—their privilege that comes with that skin color. They don't, are not sensitive to the race issues that women of color have to face at the welfare office or in the general society. We have at times tried to have conversations about it, though we've not always been successful. And we've got this piece to do. . . . I'm hoping that Sally will be able to take some leadership in and make it work.

Lastly, Eve employs gendered colorblindness explicitly when asked how issues of race have affected the group's relationship with similar organizations:

ROSE: How have issues of race impacted [the organization's] relationship with other similar organizations, nationally, or have they at all?

EVE: No. I think it's more gender.

ROSE: Gender?

EVE: Yes, nationally, some, a lot of the other organizations don't see gender issues which—primary is not the right word, *but with welfare, gender is primary since it is women who are taking care of kids.* And they just don't do a gender analysis around issues—what's the gender analysis around unemployment, what's the gender analysis around getting jobs or skill training or even being able to be active? Can't get parents to [an allied non-welfare rights organization meeting] because they're meeting at six o'clock in the middle of the week. What happens at six o'clock? Kids get dinner, they do their homework, they go to bed. I mean, and they don't offer child care and they don't have food available. So, I mean, who can participate are either people who have older kids, have another adult taking care of the kids, or don't have kids. And where's the gender analysis there?

ROSE: And that's especially at the national level?

EVE: Yeah—it's also at the local level. How do we work in coalition with other groups.

The reality of how (or whether) other organizations incorporate gender analyses is irrelevant to understanding this particular frame. This is due to the fact that Eve explicitly ranks gender as the most important factor in welfare politics in response to a direct question about *race*. While this type of frame is often coupled with clear statements about racial consciousness in terms of privilege, it is modified by the overriding need to focus on gender as a common element of oppression among welfare parents. This reflects the power of colorblindness as a racial ideology, even among social justice activists.

Gendered Colorblindness and Other Frames

Activists often utilize multiple frames in describing their political views and experiences with organizing. In the case of gendered colorblindness, two of the four activists who deployed this frame coupled it with a more general colorblindness frame, devoid of specific gendered content. In these cases, it was used to reiterate the primary point about women sharing common struggles without specifically including gender oppression in the statement. Given the relatively rare use of gendered colorblindness, it is difficult to draw conclusions about its coupling with the dominant colorblindness frame. These frames, however, are entirely compatible with each other, in contrast to the race and class consciousness frames explored in chapter 5.

Organization and Geographical Context

The story of gendered colorblindness is unique as it is the only frame deployed almost entirely by one racial group and only in one organization. This speaks to the power of racial group identity and the importance of social movement organizations in building collective identities. As the former point has been explored above, I discuss the latter point here.

Scholars of social movements have established the critical importance of social movement organizations in building collective identities.[9] What is not immediately apparent from the research at hand, however, is why only *one* organization actually encourages the usage of these frames among its members. Leadership, organizational message, and the interplay of media and racial context seem to be the primary contributing factors to this phenomenon.

Leadership
Leadership is a key factor in social movement mobilization, particularly in a small movement fractured by geographical context. While the organization in Washington State professes to be horizontally led, pockets of power are concentrated in the hands of the two full-time staff members who direct

the organization. Both of these women used the gendered colorblindness frame repeatedly in the interviews. While these leaders clearly exert considerable influence over members, it is difficult to discern from *where* these messages emerge. Further, as will be seen later in the chapter, why does this message of gendered colorblindness not resonate with women of color in the organization?

Message

In an attempt to disentangle this question of organizational influence from the use of gendered colorblindness frames by White women, I examined the "message" the group sends about itself to its active members. An analysis of the organization's newsletters—the primary means of communication with members—reveals minimal attention to issues of race and racism.[10]

I conducted a content analysis of monthly newsletters produced by the Washington State organization as well as those produced by another poverty group located in Washington, as a useful point of comparison (though this was not a statewide organization). Table 4.1 indicates that for both SMOs, but particularly for the organization in this study, race and racism were rarely discussed.

While the presence of a message from the organization about the importance of race would not, in and of itself, be enough to spur members to address this issue in the interviews, the *absence* of attention by the group does indicate an implicit approval of the relative unimportance of race. But combined with leadership and the media and racial-geographic context (explored below), this finding sheds some light on why this frame is so favored by White women in this statewide organization.

Media and Racial Context: Montana, Texas, and Washington

Both leadership and organizational message appear to be important factors in influencing the use of gendered colorblindness frames among the White women in the Washington State group. One other factor that may contribute to the usage of this frame is the coverage of poverty by the local media in Seattle, as well as the racial dynamics specific to the state itself. To gain leverage on this question of local coverage and statewide attention, I analyzed a year (March 2005–March 2006) of poverty coverage in local newspapers in three states.

These three cases were selected on the basis of both state demographics as well as organizational demographics. First, the states were selected based on poverty rates, racial composition, and racial demographics of TANF

TABLE 4.1. *Racial Cues in SMO Newsletters, 1992–2003*[a]

	Wash. State Group 1992–2003	Spokane, Wash., Group 1997–2003
Affirmative action	10	2
African American	0	1
Anti-oppression	6	1
Asian Pacific Islander/Asian American	0	1
Biracial	0	1
Black women	0	1
Caucasian/White	1	9
Discrimination	0	2
Diversiy	1	2
Equal opportunity	0	2
Hispanic/Latino	0	3
Minority	0	4
NAACP	0	1
Native American/ American Indian	0	3
Oppression	0	2
People of color	0	8
Prejudice	1	0
Race	0	5
Racial discrimination	1	0
Racist	0	2
Total	20	50
Total percentage	7.5%	18.4%

a. These numbers represent the percentage of newsletter pages that contain references to the words coded for in the table (N=268 and 272, respectively).

caseloads. Montana and Texas were selected as they share relatively high poverty rates among the fifty states in 2003 (ranked eleventh and seventh, respectively; Washington was ranked twenty-ninth), but differed in their state racial demographics. Texas is 49.5 percent White, while Montana is 89.1 percent White; the largest non-White group in Texas is Latino, while the largest in Montana is American Indian.[11] The TANF caseload in Texas is mostly non-White, while the caseload in Montana is nearly bifurcated between White and American Indian.[12] Washington State does not share the relatively high poverty rate of Montana and Texas, and is not bifurcated in terms of TANF racial demographics like Montana, nor is the majority of the caseload non-White.[13] This case diverges from the others in almost every way, while the other two share some key characteristics.

Montana and Texas also represent divergent cases on the level of individual organization. Both organizations are nearly homogenous in terms of race (one White and one African American), while both statewide organizations are relatively limited in terms of their outreach capacities.[14] The fact that both organizations are homogenous, yet different in terms of type of racial composition, offers an opportunity to investigate the politics of racial representation to the media.[15] The welfare rights organization in Washington State, however, is a relatively racially diverse organization; it provides some variance between the two other organizing contexts.

Although the advent of online news outlets has arguably narrowed the readership of local newspapers, they still reach a number of average citizens as well as policymakers in the state. Moreover, welfare rights activists in these groups overwhelmingly stated that newspapers represented the most accessible avenue for their message. While TV and radio offer a different audience as well as storytelling advantages not as available in newsprint, the activists interviewed expressed that they had a great deal more control over crafting their message in print rather than these other media. Newspapers also generally offer the opportunity for more "space" to tell stories both about welfare parents and policies. Activists also indicated that newspapers offered fruitful avenues for building relationships with reporters that were not often available in the context of radio and TV journalism.

The newspapers selected for analysis, the *Helena Independent Record*, the *Houston Chronicle*, and the *Seattle Times*,[16] represent statewide papers that are, however, localized in the particular city where these groups are based. Each paper was searched for the term "poverty" appearing in the headline or lead paragraphs of individual articles. Then this search was refined according to cues[17] that signaled race, and broken down into three categories: state/local, national, and both state and national coverage. I also coded each of the articles for general references to race.[18] Finally, articles devoted to Hurricane Katrina coverage were separated from the total so as to not distort the results. Table 4.2 attests to the relative infrequency of racial cues in poverty coverage across all newspapers. Seattle, however, surpasses both Helena and Houston in its paper's inclusion of racial cues in poverty coverage. Interestingly, the city with the most racially diverse population, Houston, has the fewest references to race in their poverty articles.

Two points from table 4.2 are noteworthy. First, although the sample size of this analysis is small, it is apparent that the coverage of poverty is

TABLE 4.2. *Articles* [a] *on Poverty with Racial Cues, March 2005–March 2006*

	Articles wtih Racial Cues	Total Poverty Articles	Percentage of Poverty Articles with Racial Cues
Helena Independent Record	19	55	34.5
Houston Chronicle	4	27	14.8
Seattle Times	9	15	60.0

a. Excludes articles about Hurricane Katrina.

a low priority for each of these papers. Further, these results may actually be *inflated* in terms of attention to poverty as the time period includes the Hurricane Katrina disaster. Second, news media attention to poverty issues presents a catch-22 situation for welfare rights groups. On the one hand, any heightened awareness of the struggles families in poverty face, particularly in cities in which these groups organize, is of benefit to SMO organizing and advocacy goals. On the other hand, the tendency for these stories to reinforce preexisting (racial) stereotypes about the poor, especially the welfare poor, is of great concern to these groups. Organizations made up predominately of women of color are at an even greater risk of being portrayed in a negative light in these types of stories. It is this dilemma that frames and constrains the choices available to organizations in their attempts to represent the realities of welfare families.

Returning to the question of gendered colorblindness–frame usage among activists in Washington State, the relatively high percentage of racial cues contained in poverty coverage may provide some insights into the question of an organization's impact on the use of particular frames. White women may be attempting to assert a "unifying" force (sexism) to counter the racialized coverage of poverty in the media that may affect their organizing efforts. While this may be an attractive short-term strategy, I argue that it has a negative long-term impact on achieving movement goals. Moreover, it creates fissures in coalitions at the national level, which are discussed extensively in chapter 7.

The three factors of leadership, organizational message, and the interplay of media coverage with racial context all appear to play some role in influencing the deployment of the gendered colorblindness frame. None of these factors alone, however, can explain this occurrence, because the other statewide organizations I studied have similar degrees of strong leadership and many have similar racial-geographical contexts. As these organizational-context factors appear to influence the usage of this frame, what is more puzzling is why women of color from Washington State do not use this frame or even explicitly reject it in the interviews. I take up this question in the next section.

Gendered Colorblindness: Women of Color

Why do women of color interviewed in this organization explicitly reject this frame? The three women of color[19] I interviewed all explicitly rejected the use of this gendered colorblindness by their own organization. In fact, they used race and class consciousness (chapter 5) frames to describe what they viewed as a weakness of this organization: the group's focus on gender to the detriment of race and, to a lesser extent, class. Without exploring the specific elements of the race and class consciousness frames each woman employs, I will detail the extraordinary similarities between the three responses.

Sue, an Asian American activist, had been a paid organizer with the organization for three years. She was deeply frustrated with racism in the organization and had recently left the group. The excerpt below is a small portion of our discussion about the racial side of welfare in the media and how it operates within the organization:

OK, first of all, quite frankly, [the organization] does not address the racial images in media. Second of all, I haven't seen much of a real thought process. Sure, on the surface, if you look at us, we have people like Shemekia or Sally or other women of color. Again, because [the organization] fails to provide any systematic thinking or education—everybody's at different levels and I know that for myself, as an example, in working with both of them. I mean, I really hate to say it, I mean, you know, 'cause everybody starts at a different level. When I moved from Hawai'i in 1983 I really had no idea, despite growing up in a reasonably diverse place like Hawai'i, what the nature of racism is, especially on the mainland. I found out the hard way because I worked in Northwest Florida for eight years for the federal government. And you can imagine that who I am, I was a little younger then and as a woman in a mostly male environment working for the Air Force I learned it the hard way. *Because without the vocabulary and the ways to describe the systematic nature of racism and the processes that go on, you are helpless.*

Sue first rejects the notion that the group deals with the racialized image of welfare in the media. As is the case in many of the interviews, she then tells a personal story to connect with the larger issue of racism and her struggles with it. She implicitly describes her experience in an "all male environment" not in terms of "sexism" but of racism, emphasizing the intersectional nature of her experience.

While Sue acknowledges the veneer of a multiracial organization, she then describes the importance of connecting racial identities of individuals with the development of systemic analyses of oppression. She not only identifies a lack of systematic analysis within the organization as a whole, but also the leadership's *deliberate* manipulation of members of color:

Just like when the [annual membership day]—that was one of my . . . OK, first of all, assessing where people were at, and then, I think *deliberately, if I might be so bold, deliberately picking people who were naïve, like Shemekia and Sally, about internalized oppression and all that that represents.* It's not that they don't know anything because obviously they're Black women, but, in terms of I would try to have conversations with them about, "hey there's a real process about doing anti-oppression work and that's really important." And Shemekia told me something like, to the effect of, I don't like to say this, because I really like her as a human being—she said, "I don't have time for it." I was lookin' at her like, you better be havin' time for it because each of us needs to have a good understanding if we're gonna go out there and do any kind of political work. I don't care who you are. Especially for marginalized people, we need to have a fuller understanding. And I'm not saying we couldn't do anything, but it's a process of education. So, you know, as far as what that might look like, I think that [the organization] does need to start from the ground up with its members because if you're not educating your members, your volunteers, your staff, and your board, then [the organization] is not going to have a coherent message or any kind of message to impart through the media. And I think that's why [the organization] really is silent because of as I say, *there's a lot of denial around—you're asking, so I'm telling you—White privilege. White privilege says that you don't ever have to actually deal with this or think about it systematically.*

Sue's recent resignation from the organization allows her, perhaps, to be remarkably frank about the institutionalized racism in the group. She details not only a denial of White privilege, but also the deliberate selection of women of color who will ostensibly "put up with" this denial in the organization. Her observations about the group underscore an important point of this type of analysis of frames: commitment to anti-oppression analyses goes beyond the racial identity of members in the individual organizations. Sue asserts that at least on paper (or in the news media) the organization appears to be multiracial. This, however, does not guarantee a consciousness about the systemic nature of race oppression. In fact, it may lead to deeper denial on the part of leadership because this cosmetic diversity enables leaders to feel that the organization is not only inclusive, but committed to an anti-oppression organizing framework.

The second activist, Mae, an African American, had been a paid organizer, welfare parent, as well as policy committee (volunteer) member for three years. She first explicitly stated that the group did not grapple with the racial side of welfare in the media. I then probed deeper to ask her about how race operated inside the organization:

ROSE: So along with that, how do you think race has impacted [the organization] internally as an organization?

MAE: Well, we seem . . . I guess they're still trying to form that anti-oppression group. I don't know what's expected out, I don't even [think] Sally knows. The whole thing about it is, what are we supposed to get out of this, what is it that we're trying to prove? You know, when we had the membership day, if they were going to come here then maybe we should have spent the whole time focusing on that. You know, they didn't get committees, they didn't get to really present it long enough and by the time we got out of the small groups we never touched down on it or . . . I don't know what they're doing with that—what they want to get out of it. I don't even know if [the organization] knows how they either want to say what they want in it, you know? I don't know. I mean the intent is there but that's hard too 'cause when you're touching down on this it's like, at what point, you're not going to be able to satisfy everybody. And if you're going to do anti-oppression, is it gonna be on race, is it gonna be on size, is it gonna be on sex, is it gonna be on class? The list goes on and on, you know? [laughs]

ROSE: Well, what do you think is important for [the organization] to address in these anti-oppression issues?

MAE: Well, I guess race could be one, class could be one, you know. [Eve, the executive director] once told me that she felt sexism was more important than race. I don't know if I agree with that. Yeah. So, you know, I don't, I don't know what [the organization] wants to do with that. And I don't even know if she's really able to tell us what she's looking for or how we would find the right person to do that. That's a very hard one.

Mae appears to question the entire attempt to engage in anti-oppression trainings without first thinking through its purpose. In addition, she argues that the group needs to articulate a clear expression of the parameters of anti-oppression work. When asked which areas of oppression were critical for the organization, she identified race and class (race and class consciousness, chapter 5). She then arguably rejected the premise of gendered colorblindness put forth in the preceding sections. She disagreed with a hierarchical approach to oppression and then reiterated her objection to an unclear approach to anti-oppression trainings. Mae, like Tara, feels uneasy with the gendered colorblindness approach so prevalent in this organization.

Tara, an Asian American woman activist with the organization for four years, had been both a policy committee and board member with the organization. Her perspective on the organization, while somewhat more cautious than the previous two activists, was nevertheless quite similar. Her tentative answer to the question of race and the media demonstrates this uncertainty about the organization's strategic choices:

TARA: I don't think we actively confront it. I think that's one of our weaknesses. I think that we've approached situations critically, you know, when depending on the article, depending on the general, like thinking about who we're gonna, we're gonna have as the person to talk to and how that will play out, you know, in the general public. But I feel like we're in a position of kind of scarcity in that we don't have a lot of parents that are available to speak to the media and so we want, at least, we don't, we'd rather them come to us and use one of our parents than just, go down to [the Department of Social and Health Services]. And it happens that a lot of our, of the women that are ready to speak are women of color. So sometimes I worry about that, about that just reinforcing the stereotype.

ROSE: So you think that in general [the organization] has problems confronting it?

TARA: Like directly . . . yeah.

Tara's concerns reflect some of the anxiousness felt on the part of White women in the organization. Once I pushed her to clarify the impact of race on the organization's internal dynamics, however, she rejected the gendered colorblindness frames of the organization as a whole:

ROSE: How do you think, well, is there anything else . . . how do you think race has impacted [the organization] internally?

TARA: I think that from what I've seen is that [the organization] is that it's a fairly White organization and that because of that perspective . . .

ROSE: Do you mean in numbers or in sort of positions of power?

TARA: Yeah, folks in power and just in general, like you walk in and see the people who are doing the work, you know, the organizers, the executive director, they've all been White, generally.

ROSE: So you mean numbers and sort of positions of power?

TARA: Yeah, yeah. Not of our membership necessarily, but of the staff.

ROSE: OK, so you see a difference between the internal part and the membership?

TARA: Uh huh. And that affects, I think just the way, like, so, *I feel like that we're really strong on the analysis or the idea of, you know, of sexism, you know, just women and of class even. But the intersection of—the intersection of—I mean the difference of women, class, and people of color, like, what happens, like bringing the analysis of racism into these things that happen, I think that that's kind of lacking.* You know what I mean? And how that, I mean it's, it's accepted and it's known I think within the office and the organization that a person of, a woman of color, her experience within the welfare system is completely different, you know, than a White person's, woman's experience. But that isn't necessarily at the forefront of our work. *Like I was saying, that we're led by the women and class issues, you know, women's rights, poor women's rights, and gender and class at the forefront, but we aren't raising race as part of the . . .*

ROSE: So you said that you think that most people are aware of the issues but it doesn't really get translated . . .

TARA: It's not like "out there," you know what I mean? And I think that's because of, the people working in the organization because there isn't somebody there saying *"wait a second, race is like huge, race is one of the huge factors, as much as sexism."*

Similar to Sue, Tara explicates the difficulties of looking only to the racial composition of membership and leadership of an organization in determining the degree of integration of antiracist analysis into organizing work. She also constructs her analysis of the organizational message in intersectional terms, referring to the emphasis on sexism and, to a lesser extent, class (women and poor women). This emphasis, she feels, erases the critical ("huge") racial component of welfare politics in the organization.

All three activist women profiled here share in their rejection of gendered colorblindness feeling a sense of erasure of self. Arguably, gender is simply a metaphor for Whiteness in the organization: Why respond to a question about race by explicitly positing gender as a more "important" shared characteristic? The erasure of difference between women through colorblindness language acts as a unifying and ultimately exclusionary tool of the voices and experiences of women of color. The discussion of intersectionality between NOW and NWRO in chapter 2 parallels, in many ways, this tension within this particular welfare rights organization. Simply claiming that an organization represents the interests of *all* women does not make it a reality. It is not a self-fulfilling prophecy. This is the core problem with organizations such as NOW, which purported to represent all women, when, as indicated by their own surveys of membership (chapter 2), they only represented a narrow group of women: straight, middle-class, married, White women. Surely these women deserved representation, but why was it to the exclusion of women who did not share these privileged identities?

How do these patterns of gendered colorblindness connect with processes of secondary marginalization? A single marginalized identity, gender, is used to simultaneously erase and separate difference. Erasure of other marginalized identities is accomplished by simply declaring "we're all women." Race is eliminated in this statement, especially if it is a *response* to a question about the importance of race. The role of class is slightly murky, although it seems to straddle both race and gender as an "enhancer" or adjective to emphasize a point. Class, when present in these interview excerpts, is a rhetorical tool to enhance an argument either for or against gendered colorblindness. In other words, the primary identity in the first formulation is gender and in the second it is race. Class enhances either argument. There are two possible reasons behind this usage. First, when compared to race or gender, class is a relatively slippery term. This is especially true in a movement where members and leaders may actually earn a similar income but be of a different "class."[20] For example, a middle-class woman temporarily experiencing divorce, domestic violence, and welfare is markedly different from a woman who has been struggling from low-wage job to low-wage job for a long period of time. Nevertheless, they may both be classified as "low-income" and have both experienced welfare. Second, class is an attractive "additive" factor to enhance an argument that "we're all the same." This facet will be explored further in the next section, on the allure of class colorblindness as a rhetorical frame for welfare rights activists.

Class Colorblindness

Welfare is a problem of class. Although this statement seems self-evident, it is actually false. Welfare is a problem of poverty, not class. TANF parents share the experience of poverty, yet their class backgrounds may be quite varied. Activists and scholars have recently begun to consider class in terms of culture, not just socioeconomic status.[21] Class as culture describes an approach that views class as a fundamental part of an individual's identity that transcends income. Analyses of class beyond income, for the purposes of this study, may be divided into two categories: class as wealth and class as culture.

Melvin L. Oliver and Thomas M. Shapiro's groundbreaking study *Black Wealth/White Wealth* pushed scholars of race and class to examine critically the gap in wealth accumulation between Black and White Americans.[22] Oliver and Shapiro argue that income is an inadequate measure of status gains by a particular racial group. First, income is a very limited tool for understanding an individual's financial position over time. Second, wealth expresses the availability of social networks critical to socioeconomic advancement. This distinction between wealth and income is particularly useful in understanding the different class backgrounds of groups of TANF parents. Some women receive TANF due to a temporary decline in income such as divorce, unplanned pregnancy, temporary unemployment, domestic violence, or some combination of these factors. For this group of women, TANF is a temporary support system until they find employment, relocate, or recover. These women may come from middle-class backgrounds, have formal education, or have economic support networks that may be able to assist them through their temporary loss of income.

Another distinct group of TANF parents are those women for whom welfare is their *only* support system. They may have grown up in a working-class family, have little formal education, and have a weak (in reference to the availability of resources) economic support network among friends and family, who may also be low-income themselves. While TANF may also be a temporary program for them, especially compared to the defunct AFDC program, it provides a safety net between low-wage jobs. For these women, poverty is either a constant, or a constant threat, throughout much of their lives.

In one sense, the joining of these two groups of women in the fight for welfare rights provides numerous opportunities for cross-class organizing. But when this underlying dynamic remains unexamined by movement activists, much like race, it can create excessive tension that undermines movement cohesion. When this dynamic intersects with race, it may create a lethal combination for movement survival. When class frames are used in combination with colorblindness, race is reduced to an outcome or subset of class divisions. I turn now to a theoretical overview of the scholarship on this problematic approach to analysis of race and racism. Following the outline of the theoretical difficulties of subsuming race under class analyses, I explore the practical organizing pitfalls of approaching welfare rights in what I term a "class colorblindness" frame.

Theoretical Approaches

Marxist approaches to race have long emphasized the essentially reductive character of race under the rubric of class analyses. Sociologists Michael Omi and Howard Winant describe Marxist approaches to the study of racism as either the product of class divisions or as an a priori enhancement of these divisions.[23] While there are multiple critiques of Marxist approaches to race or other approaches that focus on stratification—which also emphasize the primacy of class divisions—the primary critique of both rests on subsuming specific racial contexts under a general analysis of class. This general analysis does not fully explain historical and contemporary racial dynamics.[24] In the case of welfare rights organizing, this analysis is complicated by the shared class status of most of the members of this movement. These women are at the mercy of the institutionalized racism of the welfare state apparatus.

Frame Articulation

As a longtime White, antiracist organizer, Frances Kendall writes of the practical pitfalls of subsuming analyses of racism under class oppression (and, for that matter, under gender oppression): "In most of my work on white privilege I have been careful not to talk about class because I see it as a way those of us who are white escape having to deal with race."[25] Just as White women may use their shared gender identity with women of color as an "escape hatch" to ignore or minimize experiential intersectionality based on race, class may be used in the same manner. In some ways, this approach is more insidious than gendered colorblindness. This is because class, within the context of class colorblindness, is often used to describe a shared income status, not a shared class status. As discussed previously, women entering the TANF system may not share the same class background. This may change their perspective of the program and similarly their expectations of the function of the welfare system itself. Thus appeals to shared class status may not only obscure fault lines along the axis of race, but also ignore real differences in class position.

In the following sections, I explore the outlines of this particular frame. I coded responses as including class colorblindness frames if they included explicit use of "class," "economics," or "poor" in describing the group's reaction to the problem of race and welfare. The use of this language also had to include statements about class being a more important issue than race. In other words, class colorblindness frames diminish the importance of race by asserting the primacy of shared class status.[26]

Class Colorblindness: White Women

By far the most common class colorblindness frame used by White women, "ranking oppression," describes the need to order forms of oppression in a strict, linear hierarchy. In this case, class is ranked as the overarching category of oppression that all welfare parents face. This is certainly a true statement. The difference between this type of frame and what I term "race and class consciousness" is that class is used by White women as a category to suppress, ignore, or otherwise obscure the intersection of race *with* class or gender *with* class. These activists thus place racism somewhere below class as a "problem." As noted previously, this type of framing, while perhaps attractive in the near term, presents two critical problems in terms of the politics of intersectionality and welfare. First, it assumes that race, class, and gender are discrete categories that may be placed on a hierarchical plane. Second, it effectively uses one category of oppression to silence internal organizational/ movement problems of racism and sexism, and presents a "unified front" that marginalizes those women whose sociopolitical identities are the products of multiple forms of oppression.

Linda, a White activist in West Virginia, provides perhaps the best example of this frame. Similar to the other White women who use this frame, she combines it with a traditional colorblindness frame to make her point. My question about the racial side of welfare led her to describe her organization's relationship with a funder:

LINDA: She told me she's gonna ask the race question. I'm like, what? You know? And because, see, my children are African American—they're biracial. And, so, 'course my views on race—I feel we're all connected to God, I mean we're *all human beings* on the earth and you know so, I, don't really, I mean race and culture is important and ethnic at teaching—I think we should never forget if you know what your ethnic or if you're German or if you're African American, if you're Asian, I mean, whatever, you should never forget your race, of being you know who you are—*but, in society, you know, we should all work together. And it comes down to classes too, you know, rich and poor.* But [a funder] did ask about race and do we have an African American on our board? Or as members of [the organization]? And, you know, at that time we didn't, or we've had [a certain number] over the last couple of years.

ROSE: You mean on the board or . . .

LINDA: Just members. Yeah, members. And so recently I got my goddaughter—she goes to, she works, she doesn't have children and she goes to you know West Virginia, you know, Institute—and so she's African American and she became a member and then I've got two more, I'm trying to call 'em and make sure they still want to be on the board but they're young people from where I live and they're great. So, I mean, to me, I don't really, there isn't a lot of Black people here. You know, I see more of Caucasian or rural or from Appalachian background. *So, I don't really, I think it isn't really about race. I really think it's about economics.* And you know, whether you're poor or what you can better yourself and if you have that goal and you reach out and do it with determination and, you know, support or whatever America or economy or welfare or whatever program you can get at the time the better, if you go for it you can become someone in your life. *It doesn't matter your race—it's who you are as a human being.* And what you see and what you want give back to life and those around you. *So, I mean, race is important but I don't think it is, I just feel we're human beings on the earth and we're all important and that's what I try to, you know, implement and put out.*

In addition to using "we're all human" colorblindness frames, Linda describes the complex relationship between race and class in Appalachia. Her status as a mother of biracial children clearly influences her view of race and class. A number of White women in this study had African American children; it is interesting to note that Linda qualifies her description of her own children as African American with the term "biracial." This reflects the deeply personal aspect of race and welfare politics discussions and the stake individuals have in defining one another as the "other." This might help explain why Linda acknowledges the importance of race but still subsumes it as a qualifier under the rubric of economics. She seems simultaneously comfortable and uncomfortable with discussions of race; perhaps class rhetorically assists her in resolving this tension. She minimizes the importance of race in relation to class, however, without really describing how the two interact with each other.

The next example of class colorblindness asserts the physicality of race as adequate to the task of confronting racial stereotypes. Again, the importance of race is not denied, but rather assumed to "exist" when women of color are present. Alison, a White activist in Washington State, first says that her organization confronts racial stereotypes in the media. I asked her a specific follow-up question in which she admits that the issue is implied by a low-income, multiracial presence:

ROSE: OK—and you're saying though the media, or how specifically are they confronting it?

ALISON: They confront it, among ourselves, for one thing. We are able. . . . This is nothing that we tiptoe around.

ROSE: OK.

ALISON: And I'd say, you know, we've gone to our legislators and talked to them. We have mentioned low-income issues. We don't really put it in racial terms, but, not that I can think of . . .

ROSE: OK.

ALISON: But many times there's a rainbow of us going, [laughs] so by itself it does, I guess!

Similar to gendered colorblindness, class colorblindness frames were used relatively rarely by White women (only four women in Montana, West Virginia, and Washington State). They most often were independent frames; when they did overlap with other frames, it was most commonly traditional or cosmetic colorblindness. I turn now to the usage of these frames by women of color and why they represent a different type of communicative message, based on the racial identity of the interviewee.

Class Colorblindness: Women of Color

Only two women of color activists employed a class colorblindness frame in response to interview questions concerning race and welfare. References to class were sprinkled throughout the interviews, however, as was the case with White women activists. One activist who used this class colorblindness frame did so in combination with the race and class consciousness frame (explored in chapter 5), and the other used it in conjunction with race-conscious language. The use of these frames, however rare, by women of color may be viewed in a different light than their use by White women activists. This view is based on two dynamics that differentiate the two groups. First, the response by women of color may be seen as a defensive reaction to my status as a White woman interviewer. Second, it may be an attempt to assert the importance of a shared class status as a basis for organizing beyond race. In this sense, use of class colorblindness frames by women of color has much more in common with race and class consciousness frames used by both women of color and White women. The first example of use of this frame by an African American activist, Gwen in Houston asserts the importance of class solidarity in class colorblindness language. After we had already addressed the issue of race,[27] however, she stated the following:

> Well, I'm gonna tell you how we deal with it. Well, first of all, we're a low-income group and we consist of a lot of Black people, and a few Spanish people signed on, but they never come out to the organization because when they do come out they pretend like they can't speak English, OK? So let me tell you, you know how participation is in that and we're, I have answered questions about welfare and what to do and how to handle the people and I just mean Blacks, Whites as well call. They all pretty much have the same problem. *So we don't—we're not racially prejudiced 'cause when you don't have, you don't have. Low-income and poor don't have no color lines. Don't have color—that's colorblind.* We as a group. And I would employ—I would really love it if somebody of another ethnic group would come and join in and help us out, you know. Well, I can't say that 'cause Jim [White lawyer they work with] is White and he work with us. And he just like, he just like one of us, you know? He talk a little different language but we all eat the same food—he eats oxtails, we eat oxtails—he eat beans, we eat beans, so, you know, we don't have no problems with racial lines. And that's one thing we hardly—if we do discuss the issue, I'm just say-

ing if we would, we would not discuss that like they did at that [national conference]—the way they did. That would be something that would be discussed strictly between us—you know what I'm saying? You know, we wouldn't just put that on the agenda as a program. I wouldn't. I would never do that.

Gwen's statement about the group's approach to race may be viewed in two complementary ways. First, she is signaling to me, the interviewer, that I am welcome in the movement, perhaps because her group is predominantly African American. Second, she asserts the importance of class solidarity, which, if spoken from a racially privileged position, would appear exclusionary. She also asserts the need to have intra-group discussions of race in the realm of national organizing.

The only other woman of color to use this class colorblindness frame, Serena from California, explicitly used class as an overarching theme in her response to my question concerning race and welfare:

I mean we try to make everything as diverse as possible. Our groups, even in our staff, that's definitely a big thing, I mean we try to keep things at least, if we can't you know have diversity at least have understanding and have people. 'Cause there's a lot of also—when you're working with people it's very hard sometimes, like when [White organizer] tries to go do outreach especially in Oakland, [she]'s White, very obviously White, she has dyed hair and tattoos—I mean it's more of a punk rock image or something and sometimes going out into you know African American communities they're like, "Who are you?" And it's really hard to do outreach as far as that. Once they get to know her, of course, like her individual clients, it's completely different, but as far as outreach I think that's where race definitely comes in. Just into getting people to eventually come in and, you know, work with us. And then I feel like also with other organizations that's also an issue. . . . I don't know, I feel like, in my personal opinion, I think that sometimes people let race get in the way of the issue. I think it's definitely important to identify each of these struggles separately but also, I mean, I feel like before race, and especially prejudice, in regards to race, it's poverty. No matter what color you are they're gonna put that before. And people need to realize that that's kind of a way to unify everyone is that you're all low income and they treat you all the same way. After that, maybe then they start, the persons kinda get divided up depending on your race or your appearance, but I think it's class and income before anything else and that people need to focus more on that. And that's definitely a way to kind of overcome other problems.

Serena's view on race and class, unlike Gwen's view, clearly stresses the need to "get beyond race" in welfare rights organizing. This may be due, in part, to the strong class analysis in this group's organizing orientation.[28] As Serena is the youngest person (age nineteen) interviewed, her statements may also reflect a generational difference in perspectives on race and class.

Multiple Identities and Colorblindness

Gendered colorblindness and class colorblindness frames are critical to understanding the full dimensions of colorblindness as a political ideology and its implications for social movement organizing. In some respects, they are evidence of the pervasive, powerful nature of colorblindness as a racial ideology: colorblindness is able to incorporate different life experiences based on marginalized identities without changing its central message. This message is that race and racism have no bearing on the ways our political, social, economic, or cultural lives are ordered or experienced.

While these frames embody the promise of a more complex analysis of the processes of marginalization, they fall short of an intersectional perspective on the politics of welfare. Ultimately, they prove more difficult for activists to challenge given that the underlying sentiment of class and gender oppression ring true. The following chapter explores the possibilities for reordering these considerations of race, class, and gender oppression in a manner that challenges the hegemonic reign of the racial ideology of colorblindness.

Breaking Rank

Race and Class Consciousness

CYNTHIA: Love don't see no colors.
TRINA: And honey, they hate to see some of 'em colors comin' their way!

As colorblindness is the principal racial ideology of the United States, both dominant and subordinate racial groups must grapple with the contours of this discourse. Bonilla-Silva asserts that groups that challenge this racial status quo must structure their claims *against* colorblindness.[1] This acknowledgment, I argue, inadvertently legitimates an ideology itself. As the core characteristic of colorblindness is its invisibility, however, acknowledging its existence is, in itself, a challenge to the racial status quo. This type of struggle against colorblindness discourse is not limited to racially progressive actors. Indeed, White-supremacist racial ideologies based on biological or cultural superiority also call for an unmasking of colorblindness as a false racial ideology. Therefore, unveiling this discourse as anything but colorblind is not enough to create a racially progressive alternative to the prevailing ideology. It demands an articulation of the dynamics of racial oppression and an explication of their linkage with other forms of marginalization. Simply put, an analysis of power dynamics is the focal point of race and class consciousness frames.

Intersecting Marginalization

In contrast to other frames explored in this book, race and class consciousness frames *contest* the racial status quo rather than accept its ideological parameters. These frames also transform intersectionality from a theoretical approach to a practical organizing and political strategy. Traditional, cosmetic, gendered, and class colorblindness frames (chapters

3 and 4), while incorporating different facets of welfare parents' multiple identities, ultimately reduce or minimize the importance of the intersection of these marginalized identities in experiential and political terms. Moreover, colorblindness frames articulate different forms of marginalization in a hierarchical manner rather than as mutually constitutive processes. Race and class consciousness frames, on the other hand, take experiential and political intersectionality seriously. They reflect a consciousness about the multiplicative nature of identity and, by extension, the multiplicative and interlocking qualities of these systems. This chapter explores these intersectional framings of marginalization, primarily by women of color. In chapter 6, I explore the dynamics of the only organization in which both women of color and White women embrace race and class consciousness frames.

Frame Articulation

A race and class consciousness frame contains a number of related components. First, interviewees' responses were coded as race and class consciousness frames if their response to my question about race and welfare was to engage with the language of racism. Second, these frames included an articulation of race and class—or racism and classism—in an intersectional framework. Thus racism and classism were described in some fashion as mutually constitutive categories/identities. Third, these frames included a discussion of marginalization based on identity as a systemic rather than as isolated, individual, or purely situational phenomenon. I describe the subcategories of these frames in the following sections.

Race and Class Consciousness: Women of Color

In contrast to their White counterparts, women of color activists, regardless of organization, overwhelmingly favored race and class consciousness frames. Eighteen of the twenty-two women of color interviewed used these frames in describing their views on welfare and race. This suggests that organizational context may influence White women's views on race and welfare to a greater degree than it does for women of color. I explore these dynamics of experiential intersectionality in terms of race, class, and gender further in the following sections, after first outlining the various categories of race and class consciousness frames.

The Frames: Women of Color

Race and class consciousness frames, like colorblindness, have an internal logic that binds them together into a coherent narrative. The internal logic that unites these frames is critical race theory, specifically intersectionality theory, explored in chapters 1 and 2. To reiterate the central point of intersectionality theory, I turn to Crenshaw's description of political intersectionality: "Racial and sexual subordination are mutually reinforcing, that Black women are commonly marginalized by a politics of race alone or gender alone, and that a political response to each form of subordination must at the same time be a political response to both."[2] This mutual reinforcement of marginalization on the basis of race and gender also intersects with class in the politics of welfare. Crenshaw's definition also implicitly demands action on this point from political organizers. Ignoring this intersectionality not only further marginalizes women of color, but also fundamentally undermines political change efforts to combat oppression based on race, gender, or class. On the whole, Crenshaw's three types of intersectionality map well onto the race and class consciousness frames in this study. In addition to structural, political, and representational intersectionality, I include "experiential" intersectionality as it captures the critical organizing fact of personal experience with racism in the welfare system.

Structural Intersectionality

Crenshaw's perspective on intersectionality is presented in the form of legal analysis; that is, it is a bird's-eye view of the problem of multifaceted forms of oppression.[3] She identifies structural intersectionality as the convergence of systems of race, gender, and class oppression.[4] While the experience of women of color is emphasized in her conception of structural intersectionality, I chose to separate these two types of intersectionality when discussing the frames used by women of color. In constructing their responses, activists have the choice to either distance themselves from their analysis by providing relatively abstract discussions of oppression or provide this analysis through a personal story of an experience in the welfare system to emphasize their point, as explored later in this chapter. They may, of course, and often do, offer both forms of analysis. Despite the surface similarity between structural intersectionality and cosmetic colorblindness, structural intersectionality frames—race and class consciousness frames—are fundamentally at odds with each other; distancing in cosmetic colorblindness is a form of power evasion,[5] while in structural intersectionality this distancing serves to sharpen systemic analyses of power in welfare politics.

Women of color employed structural intersectionality frames relatively infrequently; this is not to say that systems of oppression were not emphasized in these interviews, but that extended abstract discussions of systemic oppression were uncommon. Two activists in particular are of note in this regard. Both women were staff members of the organization in Oakland, and both experienced the welfare system at some point in their lives. The first, Grace, an African American activist, connected her discussion of welfare and race to an analysis of Hurricane Katrina and her group's response to that tragedy: "They've been very, very connected with other advocates and advocate themselves in helping the media understand that it was a *class issue fueled by racism*. And that it has to do with accessibility. Being classed out of what you need, whether it was transportation, whether it was money, whether it was housing, whether it was food and basic water. *You were classed out by a defining factor: the color of your skin or your socioeconomic group.*" Grace provides an explicit linkage between classism and racism while also implicating her own organization's response to the disaster. Similar to many other women of color activists, Grace later provides personal anecdotes to enhance her analysis of systemic race and class oppression. Gender oppression is intertwined in these discussions as well, although usually in an indirect manner.

Jacki, a Latina activist with the same organization, provides perhaps the best example of a structural intersectional analysis. She first describes how her organization emphasizes a class analysis (sometimes at the expense of a race analysis) in response to a question about how her organization confronts racial stereotypes:

> I think that, let's see. Yeah, I think it has its drawbacks, right. I think it's really, really . . . it's really great that you could open up let's say, *La Opinion*, right, and you just saw this huge action taking place at you know in front of the governor's office and in Los Angeles and you see, you know, Asian mothers and, you know, White mothers and Latinas all wearing like you know red shirts that say: "Don't target my children." And so, I think it's great to—because I think then that adds—that adds a layer, right, to the whole, to the class element of it. *And so you're able to then challenge people's perceptions of who's on welfare, right, you then, you then challenge people's what are they called? Yeah, I mean you just challenge like the stereotype of the welfare queen, right.* You then challenge people's thoughts around like,

oh, like, you know it's only the Latinos who come here to the United States to like milk the system 'cause you then have like Asian folks who people also stereotype as like the model minority. And you have White folks who, you know, many people don't expect to be on welfare and so I think that it adds a layer of complexity to the picture. *I think, then, the downfall to then not highlighting race, is then I mean you're not, you're not then able to look at you know, beyond CalWORKs [California's TANF program], right?* Like let's look at the numbers then of, let's look at the numbers of, you know, like Black folks on CalWORKs—are those numbers lower than you know Latinas and you know, if so, then let's also look at why, right? *Let's look at the, you know, just the history of racism and you know the types of schools that you know folks have access to. So I feel like the downfall is then you don't, you yeah, how to say?*

Jacki's statement underscores how welfare rights organizing is inherently part of a larger racial/social justice project. She continues her statement by emphasizing the need for race, class, *and* gender consciousness in an explicitly structural manner:

I think it's very important to have a sharp race and class analysis that go hand in hand to be able show that CalWORKs, you know, that welfare in 1996 was not necessarily reformed but it was deformed. But also that it's, it's—*we're living in a capitalist system that then, you know, needs for racism to exist and needs for sexism to exist and classism in order for it to survive.* And so, when I think, when you just focus on class then you don't look at the system as a whole—you, yeah, you get away from looking at the system as a whole and how *all those systems of oppression are then intertwined.*

As both Grace and Jacki demonstrate, these frames most often refer to the external politics of these organizations, or the movement as a whole. Specifically, they highlight the importance of communicating this message effectively to the media, the public, and policymakers.[6] Given the abstract nature of this discussion, this emphasis intuitively makes sense in contrast to the more micro-level description of organizational culture.

Gwen, an African American activist in Houston, offers a similar analysis to Grace and Jacki, albeit one that is less abstract. She connects historical trends in social policy in Houston to make a point about race and class politics:

GWEN: Then, see, they don't know their statistics 'cause welfare, welfare as we knew it, started in the South after the Confederate War—that's when welfare started—that's why the wages are so cheap in Texas—that's when it started. But see, a lot of 'em don't know it. If they want to be fightin'—fightin' for fair wages and equal housing. And what I was going to say when I lost my train of thought talking about Allen Parkway [low-income housing]—when I signed up for Section 8, it was in 1974. And they had opened up about two hundred slots—me and my sister got up at five o'clock and we was like number one and two tryin' to get Section 8. We had to go down into River Oaks, which is an affluent White neighborhood—that's where the office was. And they never called me. You know when my number came up? 1980. 1980! That's six years later. 1980. And when it come up they was just letting me know that I was still on the list. But how I got Section 8—I moved in some modern rehab apartments that had Section 8 as their sponsor otherwise . . .

ROSE: But they wouldn't have ever let you in it?

GWEN: 'Cause it was only for White people. It was only for White people. But now, it, now when you go over to Section 8 office all you see is a bunch of Blacks—that's the way they schedule them, you know what I'm saying? 'Cause less than 100% of the population sure can't—there's always more White people than Blacks. And in Houston our ethnic makeup is entirely different. I think Houston is like 29% Black—no, 29% White, 18% Black, and the rest is Hispanic, about 65%.[7] Between us and the Hispanics—we vote—they don't, so that's why, that's why we got a little power, we vote and they don't. They are a silent majority. But when they wake up and start to vote, it's going to be hell to tell the captain. [laughs]

Ayana, an African American activist in Minnesota, connected these issues to Katrina (similar to Grace in Oakland) when I asked her about the image of welfare parents in the media. She views Katrina as an event that exposed the deep racism and classism of the United States:

Lazy people who don't wanna work. Primarily they like to stereotype it as mostly African American women because Fox News Channel is the best at puttin' this out—all these women on welfare—they got all these different babies' daddies. That's what they see welfare as. And they need to look at welfare and people on welfare as these people are hard-working families that just want the best for their families. It's not like we just decided "hmmm . . . it's eight o'clock in the morning, I think I'll go spend two days at the welfare office and apply for medical!" [laughs] It's just too much. I've had my lights off how many times in the past six months? I think I should go down there. And then they advertise it as people are double dipping who are getting like [Supplemental Security Income] benefits as well and they're like, "Well, they get so many benefits." I'm just like what kind of benefits are you gettin' bein' on welfare? What benefits are you gettin'? You're barely gettin' anything at all. You're barely gettin' by. And you know, that's the image that's portrayed as TANF families, as welfare families, is that it's the incorrect image. Because these people work hard even if they're workin' in the home takin' care of their kids cause that's the first job of any job before, you go out the home and you get a job, you at home and you a parent. And they just don't, they just can't conceive that people in the home are actually working because it's a lot of work just taking care of children. And then, hopefully, you'll have time at the end of the day to maybe take care of yourself. [laughs] *That's the image that's put out there about families on welfare and it's been the same stereotype even if you look at the whole Katrina incident. Pulled the mask right off of welfare reform, didn't it? Pulled the mask right off of welfare reform because soon as they started seein' those people who were gettin' left behind, who was it? People who was left behind before Katrina ever came along and the levees were broken,* [laughs] you know. And now they're like stereotypin' those families as "well, they just don't wanna work, they just don't wanna look for a job." You know? *Had that been a whole bunch of White, rich people they wouldn't have been cool with it. They wouldn't have even been on the roof.*

Ayana explicitly ties the media image of welfare parents to the realities of welfare—she then connects this to the specter of Katrina and larger race and class issues in the United States. Both Gwen and Ayana describe macro-level trends in terms of demographic shifts, focusing on events and policy changes over time rather than micro-level politics of their own organizations. In contrast to this type of frame, organizations are of critical importance in the next type of race and class consciousness frame, political intersectionality.

Political Intersectionality
Scholars of race and gender politics have theorized that women of color are often asked to symbolically "choose" between their race and gender identities in political contexts.[8] Political intersectionality highlights how these choices

are reflected in the organization of social movement groups. Indeed, this is the core argument of this book: women of color are not merely "another" group whose interests must be taken into account; a welfare rights movement that ignores the realties of intersections of race, class, and gender oppression fundamentally undermines its own goals (a point explored further in chapter 6). The welfare queen trope represents the intersection of these three marginalized identities: any attempt to obscure this intersection ignores the interlocking nature of this oppression. The responsibilization rhetoric at the heart of all welfare rhetoric is perhaps the most obvious representation of this problem: "African Americans," "poverty," and "women" are represented as dependent and unwilling to "work" or take responsibility for their families.

This political intersectionality internal to the welfare rights movement plays out in two ways: dynamics within organizations and between organizations. The first is perhaps the most common. Women of color are asked to "turn off" their race and then "turn it on" at key moments without having their concerns integrated into the very structure of the organization. One Asian American activist, Sue, mentioned in chapter 3, was particularly bold in using this type of frame in describing her organization's internal problems regarding racism:[9]

> People with a different life perspective, like people of color who have, how can I put it, OK, so now you're asking, so I'm answering. *[The organization] seems to have difficulty working with people of color who have a very clear analysis of race, class, and gender and how they go together.* Meaning that on the surface, I see them pick people, like Shemekia [an African American woman], who I think is a wonderful person, but she lacks a lot of information about many different areas of life. And I say that with all the best intent but [the organization] I don't see [the organization] doing the leadership development that leads to—for instance, if you're always quote, unquote scripting people when they have to go to places like Washington, D.C., to talk on the [national economic justice coalition]—that's not leadership development, you're not really teaching them how to stand on their own. The long history that [the organization] has of ignoring that every community is different. . . . [The organization's] unwillingness to deal with its own, as an organization, its racism, quite frankly, even the classism and other isms that you really need to look at—sexism. But at least those, especially the racism. [The organization's] unwillingness to acknowledge, like *I don't think they were ever serious about the anti-oppression training.* And it kills me because that's something that I care about a good deal and I think that it's really necessary. *If you're doing political work anywhere, you really*

need to form a foundation so that your members know what that is. You need to make them aware of how integral that is to the work and, for instance, I got comments when I tried to say hey, let's do an orientation for new members and as part of leadership development include some anti-oppression work, and when I used the word "required" [staff organizer], bless her, and I like her a lot, but and she's probably someone, you know, whose received assistance and doesn't like it when things are required. *Well, I'm sorry, but quite frankly, as a minority person I find that a pretty arrogant perspective, meaning that when you have privilege its easy for you to say, "You just don't, you can't require me to do anything."*

Sue outlines the complicated way in which political intersectionality operates in her organization. She not only details the contrasting experiences of women of color in a systemic way, but also points to the fact that she feels the organization is *deliberately* recruiting and retaining women of color who do not have an institutional or systemic understanding of oppression. She is also disturbed by the unwillingness of the group's White women to take anti-oppression trainings seriously. As previous discussions of race, gender, and class in other chapters demonstrate, questions of identity and power must be conceptualized in a framework that transcends simple cosmetic or demographic appearances of "diversity." This means that interrogating the surface dynamics of race and class in these organizations produces an entirely different perspective on the movement. Moreover, I argue that these internal dynamics, as I explore in chapter 7, have direct bearing on movement agenda choices and the ability of organizations to work together in an effective way.

A microcosm of this dynamic emerged through the frames of women of color in positions of power in these organizations, in the relationship *between* organizations rather than within them. When pressed to give a greater sense of how their group was situated in the state and local SMO landscape, one African American executive director, Aisha, pointed to the particular intersectional dilemmas she faced in organizing among other groups in Knoxville:[10]

AISHA: We try to get, we empower our members, we train them, we try to do, we provide media training and public speaking training and workshops and things like that so that our members are ready when the press shows up. *We also—racism is always an issue, so we discuss it all the time. It's, dismantling racism, oppression issues are always, they're woven into our campaigns at all times so all our members are aware of what's goin' on and the racial side of everything.* And especially as a Black woman, being in the executive director position, and there's not, there aren't any in Knoxville—there's like two—me and [another executive director]. And—well, she's interim director, but I think she is for [another organization]. But other than that, yeah, we're it and I'm the youngest and that in itself—ageism, that's what I call it, is a big issue here too, so it's a challenge. It's a challenge because sometimes I'll be in jeans and T-shirt and I'll go, having to be somewhere, and I'm talking to someone and they're like, "Oh you're so eloquent in your speech," and I'm like, "Well, what did you expect—that we're all dumb?!" I mean, "none of us are educated," you know, so, that's a surprise to the other side sometimes 'cause they expect one thing and they get somin' else and it always takes 'em back a couple of steps, so . . . *We handle it, I mean, we have no choice,* you know.

ROSE: So do you guys do, I mean it's woven throughout the campaigns but do you do like workshops on . . .

AISHA: Yeah, we haven't hosted one in the last couple of years but we really would like to host a workshop—it's long overdue. We would like to, and we've been talking to a few other organizations about hosting a workshop.

ROSE: And you feel like internally the organization's really got it—I mean it sounds like you've really got that . . .

AISHA: Yeah—*diversity, and it's a requirement for our board members.* They have to go through a training whether it's one that we host or—*I mean they have to and they sign sayin' that they will.*

ROSE: How does it impact your work with other organizations?

AISHA: Well, they know that we're very aware of oppression and the issues that go along with it and, well, I mean you can't be a part of [the organization] and not be a big mouth. I've learned that over the years—*sometimes it's a curse and sometimes it's a blessing, but nonetheless, people are gonna know how I feel about an issue and you know, they like it or they don't but I have, it's my duty to at least let them know, you know.* Otherwise, I'm just as guilty of just sittin' there lettin' it, you know, let things happen or you know people say things and not callin' them on it or you know, our members become empowered to do the same, they become empowered to speak up when somin' need to be spoken on.

Although they hold the same sentiment, Aisha's response to my questions differs sharply from Sue's description of the internal dynamics of her organization in Washington State. Aisha's organization has a requirement for training among board members. She directly challenges other organizations who question her competency as an African American woman in a position of power. She also notes that she feels a duty to be *active* in pointing out issues of oppression, even those that occur outside her own organization.

Representational Intersectionality

The third type of intersectional frame, "representational" intersectionality, refers to popular culture images of women of color. In the case of welfare rights, this understanding is enveloped by the trope of the "welfare queen," discussed in chapter 1. Any attempt to discuss this trope solely in terms of race or gender or class fails to capture the intersectional nature of this highly specific stereotype. Although every aspect of this stereotype is factually false, the image provides a heuristic for the public, the media, and policymakers, belying the diverse composition of welfare families.

According to Crenshaw, a representational analysis includes two elements: first, an understanding of the cultural production of these images; and second, an understanding of how discrete analyses of racism versus sexism further marginalize women of color.[11] Most often, these frames take the form of recognition of the particular racial implications of the welfare queen. Specifically, women of color (two African American activists interviewed separately, from Houston and Knoxville) were more likely to identify the racial identity of the welfare queen when asked directly to describe the stereotypes of welfare parents:

DESIREE: *The public see 'em as Black and Hispanic and, you know, the minorities as we're called. It's like, really it's like they the scum of the earth.* You know everybody that that gets TANF are—is like they frowned upon, you know.

TONYA: They think that Families First [the Tennessee TANF program] is for folks who don't want to get out here and work, who are Black or African American, they don't want to do nothing—they just want to have babies and get on welfare.

ROSE: And then in the media—what kind of images do you see—are they the same thing?

TONYA: The media the image is always somebody African American sittin' at a desk and somebody White sittin' on the other side and that's how it's basically portrayed. *It's still that good-ole-boy network down here.* Still strong.

Another facet of these frames was the connection made between racial stereotypes and broader understandings of oppression. Janice, an African American activist in Minneapolis, provides an explicit description of the racial identity of welfare parents:

> There's just the stigmas—Black, Black, just sittin' around on their a-s-s-es, eatin' bonbons and watchin' soap operas while their kids are runnin' around in the streets. And the welfare queen thing. I don't see no changes, 'specially comin' from White class, middle White guys, you know, or just people in general that are stupid, that just don't realize welfare's not a way of life. It just happens to be that's where we're at. Believe me, I would choose, if I could, not to be on it. Unfortunately, a lot of people don't see that.

Janice not only identifies the racial element of this stereotype, but also connects it to views of Whites, including a pointed analysis of class and gender. The next question asked them to describe how their organization dealt with the "racial side of welfare," in which both Janice and Ayana answered using a representational frame:[12]

> AYANA: How do we deal with the racial side? . . . I think having a committee that has people of color and showing them that not only is it African Americans but White people are on welfare, you know, it's not just one stereotype that or people that are affected by the cuts. That's the best way you can combat it, you know, and also, too, let these people know that you have an understanding of what they're doing. Because they try to use these fancy terms that you can't understand but they're talkin' about "well, we'll take this from the general fund, from the TANF and move it into the general fund"—that's a shift! You don't have to be a rocket scientist to figure that out. So, I guess that's like the best way you can try to combat that because there's always gonna be right-wing media that's gonna always put that image out there, and the only thing you can really do is to continue to fight against that stereotype and prove them people wrong that these people that the right-wing media is portraying as lazy women who are just having a bunch of babies with different fathers is untrue. That's the only way you can combat that—try to combat it every time you get a chance to, try to bring it up and correct them to let them know that they're wrong, that the stereotype is wrong. A lot of people who think that they really don't have a clue! [all laugh] They need to be educated.

JANICE: Yeah, 'cause a lot of 'em don't even know that like there's more Whites on welfare than there is Black folks or like you know, or anything like that, so it's like our group I think educates the media. A lot of 'em don't even know stuff.

In contrast to other responses to this question, Janice and Ayana say that their organization directly confronts the racial stereotypes connected to welfare. Nonetheless, they still include a general class analysis of welfare as a whole through the discussion of their organization's budget. They go further still by describing an *example* of this problem rather than leaving the discussion in generalities. Janice and Ayana describe their experiences with an attempt to "educate" the media and public about stereotypes connected with food stamps:

JANICE: Yeah, we tell [the media and public]. We just tell them. I think we educate them more than what they know, so.
AYANA: It's like the whole buying junk food on food stamps in Minnesota.
ROSE: Oh, did you guys have that?
JANICE: We had national, Fox News, 'cause [Governor] Pawlenty was tryin' to say that he was cuttin' the "fat" out food stamps. And it was funny! [laughs] It was so funny 'cause I mean, like, we just like brought it—we broke it down. We broke it down, we broke it down!
ROSE: He wanted to cut food stamps?
JANICE: He wanted to cut what you could buy with food stamps. But, see, Minnesota wasn't fallin' for that shit 'cause, a Kit Kat has flour in it—is that junk food?! [laughing] And it's like, damn, when you're on food stamps, I mean it's like, I don't know who or what or whoever use it to buy a bunch of junk food. I mean, like when I go shoppin', man I go right for meat and potatoes and beans and all that good stuff, and if I want to buy my kid a damn Twinkie or a Ho Ho, that's my business.
AYANA: Yeah, *basically what was said was feeding into stereotypes about people on food stamps.* That quote went out like all over the U.S.— every paper in the whole entire U.S. picked up that article with that quote. Fox News calls us up and they showed a small part of her interview and they did not show the [whole interview].
JANICE: She was like set up—props, signs behind her, they wanted to do like I mean, she had the whole thing and ran with it—was like look, what I think babababababa . . . [laughs] I had to say . . . I had my posters and stuff up—they pulled them down when I went to

the bathroom and then they wanted to do this whole-day segment thing with you—like, "OK, we want to . . . "

ROSE: See your average day?

JANICE: Yeah, we want to see you get your kids out of bed, what you feed them in the morning and then sending them off to school and then we want to go grocery shopping with you. They spent the whole frickin' day with me. And then they only showed like this little bitsy clip—it was just of me shopping—they showed that part and I said, you know just because I get food support why should I have to shop on the other aisle? 'Cause they were tryin' to have it to where there was gonna be food that you could buy only while you were on food stamps, and then this is where you would have to get it from on this side of the aisle versus what the people . . .

ROSE: You mean like actually have a separate aisle?!

JANICE: They were gonna segregate it. They were tryin' to do it.

ROSE: Oh my God.

JANICE: Yeah! Yeah! And the grocery stores and stuff they were like, we ain't havin' that—we don't wanna do that.

ROSE: Yeah, can you imagine all the extra work for them to do that?

JANICE: They said—that was just too much. *That's a little too racist.* Pawlenty's like all, "I'll cut the fat out of food stamps!" He's fighting obesity! [laughs]

ROSE: So what you're saying is that not only do you guys think about this when you deal with the media, but you go out and directly attack it.

JANICE: Heck yeah.

Janice and Ayana's description of their media campaign highlights an awareness not only of the actual concrete impact of food stamp cuts—and the segregation of food stamp food by aisles in the grocery store—but also a targeted sense of the racial implications of the governor's attempt to reinforce the racial stigmatization of welfare parents. Their narrative of this issue also highlights the dangers of negotiating media coverage, particularly television coverage, which is easily manipulated to reinforce preexisting stereotypes.

Experiential Intersectionality

As frames describe the way in which activists puzzle through various challenges presented by organizing, they capture both abstract and concrete analyses of daily life. I have created the category of "experiential intersectionality" to capture this latter point. In contrast to other social movements, welfare rights leadership is rooted in the wisdom of welfare parents, not "experts" who may be insulated by their class and race statuses. Therefore, these experiences are often narratives through which more abstract or structural analyses of marginalization are articulated. In fact, this type of race and class consciousness frame is by far the most pervasive, and, I argue, the most critical to building the movement. It is precisely this convergence of systemic analysis with daily experience that binds movement activists in recruiting members, retaining leaders, and connecting with one another in a productive political capacity.

Trina, an African American activist in a tiny former coal-mining community in Appalachia, relates her own experiences with the welfare system and race. She includes both a race and class analysis in her response to my question about race and welfare:

ROSE: How do you think the average person views—looks at welfare families. What do you think they think of them?

TRINA: They think of, just like, they don't care, they think they're just poor people, you know. They, how would it—it just like they don't exist. They just say, "Well, we have to put them on welfare 'cause they don't have nothin'. . . . We have to take care of 'em." I don't know. And when your kids go to school and you have to dress different from other kids they know that you on welfare. 'Cause you have to get food vouchers to eat and stuff and you don't pay like other kids. I mean to me, they just, like you just—there. Just one headache.

ROSE: You're just a number?

TRINA: You're just a number.

ROSE: Are there stereotypes?

TRINA: *I think Blacks have it more harder than Whites. I do, I really do. I think they give what they can to the Whites and they let and most of the Whites find out what they can get and they let others know what they can get and they can get more. I still say they do, I'm not tryin to be, I'm not prejudiced.*

ROSE: No, you're not being prejudiced!

TRINA: But, I mean, they do! *They give 'em [White people] more food stamps, they give 'em more money, they help 'em heatin' and whatever, air conditioners or whatever, windows. . . . And they'll tell you they don't* have that program or whatever when you go over there for. One person might come out and say we got this from the welfare department. And you already tried it, you know. But I do think that they just say you're a number, you know. You're a charity case.

ROSE: If you ever see stories in the TV or in the paper about poor people or specifically about welfare families what do the stories say? What's the tone?

TRINA: They're just puttin' 'em in a poor class, you know. Like I said, they don't acknowledge welfare people to me, they don't. And, I mean, and you have people that, *middle class or upper class or whatever, they look down on poor people, you know. Even they're, even if some of 'em not poor, but the poorest poor they do look down on 'em.* And they give 'em a hard time, you know. They can't get nothin' or try to get nothin'. They turn 'em down at the banks, they turn 'em down, you know for credit, you know, they don't get nowhere. They just don't get nowhere. You say "welfare" you know, "Hey, *you ain't got nothin', you ain't gonna get nothin'!*" Not even with a cosigner! [laughs]

Trina explicitly identifies racial discrimination in the welfare system based on her own experience and those of others around her; she then broadens this anecdotal evidence out to an analysis of race and class. As with all race and class consciousness frames, interviewees will often link discrimination in the welfare system to patterns of discrimination experienced in other areas (e.g., experiences with the banking industry).

Further, these examples of discrimination in other areas often led to an extended conversation about racism and classism in the communities in which these women live. In the case of Trina and her friend, Elaine, also a member of the welfare rights group, the discussion of race and welfare prompted just such a conversation about race and class. I include a portion of this extensive conversation between myself, Trina, and Elaine. On a methodological note, I, as the interviewer, only used the phrase "racism" after the interviewees had discussed this themselves so as to avoid problems of interviewer impact on choice of words:

ELAINE: Seems like Black people always down [at] the bottom in this country.

TRINA: That's what I was tellin' [Rose].

ELAINE: I think if you don't understand—you can't walk in my shoes until you walk in my shoes . . .

TRINA: *Racism. It had to be there.*

ELAINE: Like if you said, if you in denial, then you think everything you're doin' is OK.

TRINA: It doesn't make it right. . . . I was tellin' her how pretty those White people's homes are up on the ridge. They had more opportunity than Black people when nine out of ten married somebody out of college. They went to college. I told her I said nine out of ten, yeah, their parents probably helped 'em too, you know with land or whatever, but the Black people . . .

ELAINE: Don't own land. We don't own land.

TRINA: We don't own land. And they never had the opportunities like some of these people does. 'Specially them people that lives up [the ridge] . . .

After this exchange, Elaine and Trina related stories about intimidation and bomb threats they experienced in their tiny Appalachian community. In particular, Elaine's attempt to move to the White part of the community provoked a violent response. As a result of these and other incidents, the group organized an antiracism day in the town to confront these issues. The racial tension in the community was simultaneously exacerbated and obscured by class issues and physical separation by race and class.[13] The fact that these tensions spilled over into the daily lives of town residents presented both immediate opportunities and challenges for community organizing. I now turn to how these deeply personal and political issues are double-edged swords for social movement organizations.

Uncovering Intersectionality

The experiential intersectionality described by Elaine and Trina, while offering the critical link between analysis of structures of marginalization and daily individual and collective experiences, also complicates organizers' task of popular education. Popular education refers to the notion of education starting from ordinary people's daily lived experiences as a prism to provide systemic analysis of those lived experiences. If one's daily experiences do not superficially resemble these analyses, however, an organizer's task becomes markedly more challenging. Life is never as simple as abstract analyses of oppression, as Grace, an African American organizer in Oakland, describes:

ROSE: I was just asking about race and welfare and what you see sort of on a daily basis—connect up with that. And do you see it—it's interesting to ask different folks about it—the welfare office—how do you see that playin' out?

GRACE: Well, God, I see it at so many levels. *People think race is clear-cut. Black, White. Brown, Yellow, you know. Black against White. Brown against White. No, you know, it's inter-racism. I have experienced more racism with a Black welfare-to-work counselor than I have a White because there's so many dynamics to play.* You know, when you see me, you see that I talk sensibly, so "why don't I go out there and get a job—why are you sittin' up here on an exemption when you need to get out there and work. You can work. I see mentally challenged people work—you get out there and work, you know, I'm not goin to make life easier for you." So, I, you know, *I see the effects of racism. That the propaganda of racism at play at the social services office. I do see that sometimes they use their yardstick for success by color of skin.* But, I also see the yardstick of success by social affiliations. If I know you and you grew up in Oakland for years, I could not do anything in that program and still skate through if I know that social worker and friend. And that's Oakland. It's all about affiliations and I see the mentality of it: let's play the system for certain people and for certain people, screw 'em. *Sometimes it's defined by color of skin, sometimes it's not. But it's still racism. It's still classism.*

ROSE: You mean structurally?

GRACE: Structurally.

ROSE: I don't want to put words in your mouth.

GRACE: Yeah, but that's what I meant.

ROSE: So, on an individual level you wouldn't necessarily see it unless you had some sort of analysis—know that that's what's going on—is that what you're saying?

GRACE: Yeah. If you came from Sacramento and looked at it, on paper, because paper is what they go by—they have no experiential feelings or attachments, then you would not know there's racism. If you had the demographics and you see that, you know, Susie Q., twenty-five years old, African American—she is in the welfare-to-work program, she's going to school, she has all her books paid, and then you saw Millie G., twenty-five years old, Caucasian, not getting her books, IRP [Individual Responsibility Plan] on time— whatever; been sanctioned [cut off TANF] a couple times—you'd think, OK, well, you know, Millie G. thinks she's privileged: this program's working. The underprivileged gettin' what they need; Millie G. is not gettin' what she needs because Millie G. isn't doin' what she's supposed to do. But you don't see that Millie G. has sent in the paperwork, done got lost several times, done called the caseworker—caseworker not respondin'. So it looks good on paper. But racism is definitely occurring there. Classism is occurring there, you know. Even maybe she has a Black caseworker that feel like, "Oh, well, she has all the advantage in the world, I'm gonna screw her over!" But it's still racism. And Millie G. is just as impoverished and her child may be stuck in poverty because she's not gettin' what she needs to break the cycle through higher education. So you know, it's being played out.

Grace describes two levels of "ignorance" (for lack of a better term). First, on the level of government officials, the cosmetic diversity of the welfare system on paper (in terms of employment in the bureaucracy) belies the underlying structural racism occurring at the office. Grace attributes this to the higher-level social service employees who have little to no experience being on the receiving end of the system. Second, the welfare parent entering the system for the first time (with perhaps no perspective on the broader political/institutional patterns of welfare politics), actually may have a similar perspective on the system as the government official, but for entirely different reasons. If an African American woman enters the welfare office in Oakland, Houston, or Knoxville, they have a fairly good chance of being assigned another African American caseworker. This may obscure the fact that they are still experiencing racism and classism on an *institutional* level. It is precisely this disconnect that both welfare bureaucrats and welfare parents experience that creates special challenges for welfare rights organizations. Efforts to open social service employment to African American women have the paradoxical effect of obscuring structures of institutional racism from the perspective of welfare parents entering the system. If a welfare parent's only contact in the welfare office is a woman of color caseworker who wields a great deal of direct power over her family, it may be difficult for an organizer to convince this parent that institutionalized racism structures the welfare system itself. Moreover, as Desiree, an African American activist in Houston explains, the entire system is degrading; sometimes it is difficult to perceive that someone might be treated even more poorly than you are:

It's a two-way street. You want respect, you give respect. So, I mean, I'm not, I don't know. *'Cause regardless of color, if you respect me, I'll respect you, you know? But I guess most people don't see it that way.* They come in [to the office] and, you know, maybe they ask too much or want too much, but, I don't know. I know the people over there on Scott Street [welfare office] [laughs] and *they don't care what color you are, they talk down to you period, talk rude and nasty to you, so. And it doesn't matter what color they are—they talk, all the workers talk to you like that.*

Although Desiree is African American, her response highlights one possible reason why so few White women in this study employ race and class consciousness frames. Not one of the women (of any race) interviewed had ever had an even remotely pleasant experience at the welfare office. Some caseworkers may have demonstrated more respect toward parents than others, but it occurred in the general context of a depressing, stressful, and dehumanizing environment. Even when activists understood the pressures low-level caseworkers faced in terms of bureaucratic constraints, this did not diminish the demeaning experience of the welfare office.

This pervasive feeling among welfare parents of anger and frustration with caseworkers cuts both ways for welfare rights organizers. On the one hand, this universal dehumanizing experience offers possibilities for bridging diverse groups of women. On the other hand, the very nature of the dehumanizing experience makes it more difficult to comprehend *worse* treatment on the basis of race (or class) status. Unless this experience is contiguous with other forms of discrimination one faces because of racial identity, those who are racially privileged may find it difficult to accept that racism is integrated into the welfare system. This can lead to tension in the creation of "hierarchies of oppression," a game that often plagues social justice movements. This type of discussion leads to comments such as "I am oppressed *too!*" Frances E. Kendall refers to this as the "Pain Olympics."[14] This hierarchy of oppression, implicitly expressed in color-blindness frames, is the antithesis of an intersectional analysis. It assumes discrete categories of identity as well as discrete categories of marginalization based on those identities. It is entirely unproductive from an intersectional perspective because it obscures the ways in which these identities are interlocking and mutually constitutive. It also assumes that progress for one subgroup, such as White women, necessarily translates to progress for the entire group (an error of the second-wave, mainstream women's movement, as I argue in chapter 2). Further, this perspective denies the possibility that progress for one subgroup may actually further marginalize an intersecting subgroup.

Race and Class Consciousness: White Women

In contrast to the other frames explored in this book, White women almost universally rejected the use of race and class consciousness frames. Only four out of the twenty-seven White women interviewed used these frames in their discussions of race and welfare. As their use of the frames does not follow a particular pattern, I discuss them individually. Organizational affiliation appears to play a critical role in whether these White women employed these frames; all except one are activists in the organization headquartered in Minneapolis. I discuss the implications of this organizational dynamic after outlining the dimensions of these frames as used by White women.

Gina, a White activist and welfare parent from Washington State, had been active with her organization for three years. Soon after our interview, she joined the board for approximately a year, after which she resigned and left the organization due to some of the underlying problems discussed in our interview. Much of the interview focused on racial issues within the organization. I excerpt lengthy portions of her responses as they provide a clear illustration of race and class consciousness frames. This excerpt begins with her response to my question about how her organization grapples with race and welfare (particularly in the media):

GINA: Not very well at all. And I'd say detrimentally.

ROSE: How so?

GINA: It's not a top issue. And the people that tend to be involved with the media don't necessarily reflect diversity, cultural diversity at least. So, I'm definitely not saying that every single person who participates in media activities with [organization] is White, but it's definitely disproportionate.

ROSE: To the membership base or to?

GINA: The membership base and then the members who are involved with the media. So, who is writing articles, whose names are being attached to articles, who is speaking with the media. Shemekia [African American member] and I went on John Carlson [conservative radio talk show].

ROSE: You guys did? I missed that!

GINA: Oh God. It really, it like, it was an irresponsible pairing. Like, a lot of feedback I got was like, that was a setup knowing who his audience is and knowing his style of interviewing and interaction. And when we talked about it, where we were at—in our position. And it was, like, Shemekia was the Black woman, and I was the White woman in college. Here was the Black woman getting her GED. And like, it underscored so many of the stereotypes. . . . And we were supposed to be like. . . . But in the context of the interview and the interviewer it was just like this . . .

ROSE: And you kind of felt like you were set up for that?

GINA: *I don't think it was deliberate, but I don't even think that it was understood,* or considered that was going to be a dynamic and that our differences in that context were not appropriate as representing what we were talking about, and we didn't organize with each other to even consider that because it was so last-minute—"Oh, and Shemekia's going to be there too," and, OK, that's great, I want Shemekia to be there, but then—yeah . . . it just did not happen well or responsibly, I don't think . . . *I've never seen people of color's concerns specifically addressed by people of color with a link to [organization] in general.*

Gina's response is not only race conscious in that she does not shy away from discussing race, but also in that she openly discusses how these racial dynamics affect her organization's media strategy. She recognizes not only the stereotypes of African American women, but also how her *own* position as a college-educated White woman affects this dynamic. Moreover, she is clear that there is a lack of consciousness in the organization itself when she says that the hazards of this pairing on the radio show were not "understood." When I turned to the question of how this racial dynamic affected the organization internally, she incorporated a systemic analysis of oppression, a key feature of this race and class consciousness frame:

GINA: Is Shemekia [an African American member] still employed here? [sarcastically]

ROSE: She used to be.

GINA: Yeah, *the one employee of color resigned, specifically for that lack of addressing those issues, the issues of oppression and of people of color and how they relate to the welfare system.* And internally there's always been a big disparity racially in the organization which when you consider the organization is located in a historically, like this neighborhood is historically a neighborhood of color and even though it's being gentrified it still is a neighborhood of color—the welfare office up the street primarily serves people of color. It's within walking distance of that place and yet you don't see that in the organization. You see this organization trying to reach the entirety of Seattle. That's important but then, it's, it's presuming mobility when it doesn't tackle where it's at first and get a member base and it's never done that. Or, I don't know if it's ever done that—it's not here now.

ROSE: So, you're sort of saying, reaching beyond where it needs to reach and it needs to start . . .

GINA: Or, it's like if I'm here, [visually pointing] and I want to reach here, what's necessary to do that—a lot of mobility and people to actually carry out that work. So, if I'm here, I want to try to spoke [motioning by drawing a bicycle in the air] out and like have a group of people working at home, where you're at, then when you try to go out, you actually have people to go out to this stuff, to mobilize everybody. But, it's like, we try to get together with people from North Seattle and Gig Harbor and Vashon Island and South Seattle, and Everett—not Everett, but . . . all these places and then we're "it." You know, we're at the policy committee meeting and we're not delegating or thinking of ideas to bring back to the member base. We try to think of ideas that we can do, or put out on the listserv to a kind of anonymous member base. So, it's like, where are the people that are need to do all of this stuff? And that's what I mean by working from home—the people are right here—they're all around us and . . .

ROSE: OK . . . anything else?

GINA: Yes—right on that. I was just thinking about that, why is that? And I've noticed a *trend in the organization as blaming those people for why they're not here.* That and looking at, from an organization standpoint, why don't we have a bigger member base, why don't we have a bigger member base of color is that—*I've heard a lot of "theys," or "they don't this," or "they don't . . . " which shows you that the organization isn't really ready for having those conversations. Internally, there are things that need to be addressed.*

Gina's response ties internal staff issues to membership and then to the broader socioeconomic/racial context of the neighborhood in which the organization is located. Again, this response demonstrates a consciousness about geographic context (e.g., gentrification) that implicates *power.* Moreover, Gina takes the general welfare politics dynamic of "blaming the victim" and uses it to interrogate her own group's supposed practice of racial intro-spection. Gina was the only White member interviewed in this organization who used these race and class consciousness frames; I now turn to the frames used by White women in another organization, where both White women and women of color used the language of race and class consciousness.

The White women activists in the Minnesota organization all used the language of race and class consciousness. Although I discuss the impact of geography and organizational structure in greater detail in chapter 6, it is worth noting here that these White women all have different educational backgrounds. This factor is important in reference to the patterns evident in the discussions of traditional and cosmetic colorblindness in chapter 3. Although it is difficult to pinpoint the exact class status of interviewees, there was a pattern of more highly educated, White women preferring cosmetic rather than traditional colorblindness frames. Formal education is not a proxy for class status, but it is an important facet of class background. In the case of this Minnesota organization, White activists' formal education backgrounds ranged from not completing high school to earning a college degree. I argue that race and class consciousness cuts across class; it does not rely on a "sophisticated" explanation of systems of oppression. Indeed, Lau-rie, who has been with her organization for over six years, demonstrates how personal experience—rather than abstraction—is translated into a race and class consciousness frame. I excerpt her response at length, as it is necessary for illustrating how she views her experiences in relation to parents of color struggling with the same welfare system:

> LAURIE: Well, that's another thing. You know, like, for instance, I've never had any problems, with, OK, like, if, OK, this is an example. Not too long ago I had to have some paper in to keep my medical coverage, my medical assistance, so I had to turn in some papers on—by the eighth. OK, so I knew that I was gonna be down at the welfare office on the eighth because we were petitioning there on that day. So I wanted to bring it in and hand it in personally to make sure that they had everything and everything's right and all that. So that's what I did. Then I called and I made sure, double-checked, dada-dadada, you know, I got all my stuff, "Yeah, 'Oh, no problem.'" And then I get a note in the mail. I wouldn't know. What happened was I went to get my prescriptions and they said that my medical had lapsed. And I said, "Excuse me, I'm poor, I have asthma, I have to have my medication. . . ." *But I've noticed that people of color—they*

give these people a lot of grief. They give 'em a lot of grief, like Anika, she's part of our core and she's, the same thing happened with her medical and they didn't take care of her stuff immediately—she was off it for like a month and a half or something. It took her like a month, a month and half to get back on her medical.

ROSE: Oh, so you mean they're giving her more of a hard time.

LAURIE: Right! It seems like they're giving people of [color], you know, a little harder a time. I mean I might be wrong, I mean it's just, yeah, they do. They do though and I don't know, I don't know. *It's not right. I think there's a lot of racis[m] that goes on, because they think, "Oh, the Black people are on welfare, they're lazy, they don't want to work." Excuse me!* There are a lot of prejudice in the whole world when a lot of these people try to go get a job but they don't get hired. . . . And the way I see it too, I don't care if somebody has, went to school for four years, or however many years and had to pay for their education. They, those people have to realize themselves, yes, they worked hard, but they're also privileged. God created them strong with intelligence and gave them opportunity and they should consider it a blessing. Those people should be willing to help other people, you know. They shouldn't look at this stuff, well, I'm privileged, I have a better job than you, I have a good education, you're no good because you don't have an education, you can't get a job or whatever—that's not right. There's too much prejudice in the world, people have to, you know. It's just—it's not fair, you know.

Laurie begins by juxtaposing her enormous difficulties with the welfare system to those that people of color face in the same system, and she links it to other members in her organization. The second portion of her response then broadens to a picture of how African Americans are viewed in relation to welfare. She not only notes that this image is incorrect, but also matches it with broader patterns of discrimination in hiring and to the concept of privilege in general. Privilege, in her description, includes a number of socioeconomic factors (jobs and education), although not in a context in which class erases or overrides racism, as is in the case of class colorblindness frames. As a follow-up question, I asked her how the organization dealt with these issues as an internal matter: "If there's anybody that is racist in the committee, they sure ain't gonna say it. You know what I mean?" This response was similar across all activists in this organization. She explicitly uses the language of *racism*, not *race*, to describe her group's approach to this problem. The responses of the other two White women in this organization to this internal question are explored in depth in the following chapter, about the impact of organizational context on the development of race and class consciousness frames.

Identity and Experience

Structural, political, representational, and experiential intersectionality frames employed by women of color in this study underscore the importance of identity in translating experiences into organizing strategies. As few of the White women in this study use race and class consciousness frames, it is difficult to sort out what prompts these few women to reject colorblindness language in their work. Perhaps the most productive perspective on this question is to ask why *any* White women use this frame, given its ubiquity among women of color and absence among White women. What factors might point to possible mechanisms underlying this usage by these four White women? I turn to an examination of geographic and organizational context in the next chapter to point to possible explanations.

Crossing Over

Rethinking Movement Organization

ROSE: I'm gonna ask you about the strengths and weaknesses or challenges for the group. So what are the
big strengths?

JANICE: Would you mess with us?

What do organizations in which both women of color and White women cross the divide between colorblindness to race and class consciousness look like? As a starting point, I compare two similar welfare rights organizations in Minnesota and Washington State, attending to geo-racial context, political landscape, organizational context and structure, political ideology, and internal racial dynamics. The Minnesota organization presents a unique model of an organization able to move beyond the colorblindness mind-set among White women explicated in chapters 3 and 4. Both organizational structure and racial composition of leadership are critical factors in the development of a collective race and class consciousness among the women in this organization. The features of this group lead to a broader question about the professionalization pressures on small SMOs, where technical expertise is ostensibly needed to pursue incremental policy change. I revisit Piven and Cloward's classic *Poor People's Movements*, with particular attention to their analysis and involvement in the welfare rights movement, as a way to gain purchase on the broader questions of the purpose and goals of social movements with regard to racial, economic, and gender justice. I focus here not on the periods of movement mobilization, but rather the long periods of "in-between" when activists struggle to protect the gains the movement made at the height of its leveraging of power. I argue that a more expansive view of social movements as generative of new movements and broader social change—as opposed to existing primarily for the purpose of securing incremental changes in policy—is reflected in the organization built by women in Minnesota. This perspective allows for a refocusing of movement energy on the interconnectedness of issues of social justice, which necessarily entail a genuine challenge to dominant ideologies of colorblindness and a commitment to race and class consciousness.

Comparing Contexts

The one shared factor among the White women who use race and class consciousness frames is their geographic and organizational context. With only one exception, all these women belonged to a multiracial, low-budget welfare rights organization in Minneapolis. Moreover, all the White women in this organization used these frames. Their involvement with the organization ranged from five to fifteen years and their formal educational level ranged from not completing high school to earning a college degree; all experienced welfare at some point in their lives.

As the background of these activists does not appear to offer any particular insight into their use of these frames, I argue that their organization, in and of itself, is a primary contributor to this perspective. Granted, given the deep involvement of these women in the organization, it is possible that they are the ones who shaped the organization in this way, but there is little to suggest that they accomplished this on their own. This comparison illustrates how racial-political geography and, most important, the structure of the organization underlie this trend in the appearance of colorblindness in these organizations.

Minnesota and Washington

I compare the political, racial, and economic context of Minneapolis and Seattle as a method of teasing out possible underlying factors for differences in use of frames between the two groups. Rather than compare Minneapolis and Minnesota with all the other cities and states included in this study, I select Seattle and Washington as they share a number of similar key characteristics. In terms of organizational demographics, only the California organization is comparable, though California has dramatically different racial and socioeconomic demographics compared to Minnesota and Washington (table 6.1).

Therefore, I examine the political and organizational dynamics in Washington State and Minnesota in an attempt to understand why two similarly situated organizations do not use the same frames. In later sections, where appropriate, I draw broader comparisons between the Minnesota group and the other organizations included in this study.

TABLE 6.1. *Poverty Rates and Race by State, 2003*[a]

	African American	American Indian	Asian American	Latina/o	White American
California					
Poverty Rate: 13.4%					
% of Total Population	6.2	0.8	11.9	34.6	44.8
Minnesota					
Poverty Rate: 7.8%					
% of Total Population	3.8	1.1	3.5	3.2	87.2
Washington					
Poverty Rate: 11.0%					
% of Total Population	3.3	1.2	6.4	8.0	77.8

a. American Community Survey 2003. The estimate totals in this category do not add up to 100% for the following reasons: The category Latina/o may be of any race. The White American category includes those people who identify as "White Alone, Not Hispanic or Latino." The other racial categories are single-race categories (e.g. "Asian Alone"), but may include Hispanic or Latina/os. These percentages also exclude the following alternative racial categories on the American Community Survey: "Native Hawaiian and Other Pacific Islander Alone," "Some Other Race Alone," "Two or More Races," "Two Races Including Some Other Race," or "Two Races Excluding Some Other Race, and Three or More Races."

Political Landscape

In many respects, Washington State and Minnesota share a similar political tradition: they each have a long history of progressive politics and share the same geographical splits between one large, liberal urban center (Seattle and the Twin Cities) and the relatively rural, conservative remainder of the state. Berry, Ringquist, Fording, and Hanson developed scales of both citizen and state government ideology, as party is often a less accurate measure of ideology across states.[1] In terms of citizen ideology, Minnesota and Washington citizenry are both split on a liberal-conservative spectrum: in 2003, Minnesota scored 48 and Washington 54 on a 0–100 scale, with greater values associated with greater liberalism.

In terms of political party and ideology in state government, however, the picture is more complex. Washington State tends to be more Democratic, with this party controlling the governor's office since 1985, while Republicans have held the Minnesota governorship since 1991, save for a four-year third-party interlude (1999–2003).[2] The Washington State Legislature has been narrowly divided with Democrats generally retaining control, while in Minnesota the House has been more mixed and the Senate has remained firmly Democratic.[3] According to Berry and colleagues, the *ideology* of these two state legislatures is quite different. Washington State's legislature is more liberal (72 out of 100) than its citizenry, while Minnesota's legislature is markedly more conservative (23 out of 100) than its citizenry. This could indicate that activists in Minnesota are energized by a legislature that seems out of step with the people, while in Washington activists may prefer less confrontational tactics given the relatively liberal stance of the legislature. It is difficult, however, to disentangle the directional impact of this ideological environment in organizing. Even if one were able to do so, it would be difficult to connect this with the political goals and strategies of these organizations: a more conservative legislature may spur protest on key issues when groups are threatened, or, conversely, it may dampen action due to the absence of a feeling of political efficacy.

Organizational Context

Given the relative comparability of political environment of these two welfare rights organizations, I interrogate the structure of these groups as a method of teasing out possible reasons for this split in frame usage. Moreover, as the Washington State organization is comparable in terms of frame usage by White women to all the other organizations in this study, this section seeks to explore why the Minnesota organization is an outlier in this respect. I examine the organization's resource base, political ideology, racial makeup, and internal racial power structure in conjunction with the organizational power structure itself.

Obtaining equivalent documentation and information across these organizations was quite difficult given varied individual organizational capacity. One concrete point of comparison across organizations that I was able to document, however, was their annual budget size (table 6.2).

In comparison with other nonprofits in the United States, these organizations obviously rank quite low in terms of their resource base. All are 501(c)(3) organizations, with the exception of the groups in Texas and Minnesota. The Texas organization does not have tax-exempt status. The Minnesota group has a fiscal sponsorship relationship with a church, which allows it to operate as a completely independent organization. Both of these

TABLE 6.2. *Annual Budget and Staff Capacity by State Organization*[a]

State Organization	Annual Budget	Paid Staff
California	$337,178	8
Washingon	$250,847	3
Montana	$219,727	4
Virginia	$99,821	3
Tennessee	$97,861	2
West Virginia	$54,009	2
Minnesota	$50,000	0 (apprentice)
Texas	$275	0

a. All information in this table was gathered from IRS tax returns (2004) and interviews with organization staff and members. Therefore, the date range is approximately the same as the dates of the interviews (2003–2006).

organizations also have the smallest budgets of the organizations included in this study. Unlike every other organization, activists in Minnesota were the only interviewees who felt that their budget was more or less adequate in size. I asked every interviewee to provide a "wish list" of items for their organization. The responses varied greatly across organization, but only the activists in Minnesota were cautious about how unlimited funding might affect the fundamental character of the organization, as Janice, a Minnesota activist, explains:

ROSE: If you guys had more resources or money what would be your priorities?

JANICE: We would have more problems. The more money we see, the more problems we have.

ROSE: Tell me more about the problems.

JANICE: You know, I mean, it'd be good to have more money, it'd be good. I think the, you know, if we had more resources and more money I know our group would definitely put it to use the right way. 'Cause we don't, we don't mismanage nothin'. I mean for us to like, for us to splurge, like would be to like have pizza for our committee meeting, you know what I'm sayin'? Or to rent a van [laughs] and go up to Duluth for a conference or somethin', that's a splurge for us, you know what I'm sayin'? So I know all the money would be definitely, we'd probably. . . . I don't know what we'd do.

ROSE: When you say it would make more problems, what do you mean?

JANICE: I was just jokin'—I don't think we'd have more problems. I think, I know we would put the money to good use—we would—real good use.

Although Janice says she is joking about the "problems" money would create, her response is markedly different from activists in other organizations. Her requests, like others in the organization, are relatively modest and small in scope; they would not potentially change the mission or operating structure in the way that hiring staff might. This fact, coupled with organizational operating structure, offers some insight to these potential differences in frame usage by activists.

Organizational Structure

Perhaps the most surprising contrast between the Minnesota organization and the Washington State organization—and other organizations for that matter—is their approach to organizational structure, rooted in their resource base (or lack thereof).[4] The most common response to the resource question I posed in the interviews was a request for either higher staff salaries or the hiring of additional staff. Broadly, all the "wish list" items interviewees identified fell into the following organizational capacity categories: (1) administrative, (2) geographic, (3) coalition, (4) technology, (5) services for members, and (6) specific issue/policy campaigns. The Minnesota organization is the only group (with the exception of the Texas organization) that did not have any paid staff, and, notably, they did *not* want to hire staff, even if additional resources were available. The daily tasks of the organization were taken on by volunteers (only low-income people) or "apprentices," current or former welfare parents hired to learn organizational tasks for a six-month term. This approach to organizational structure was not merely the by-product of scarce resources; it was a conscious choice that the members made with regard to the power structure of the organization. Instead of the ubiquitous nonprofit structure of an executive director responsible to a board of directors, decisions are made by a group of low-income activists who are not paid for their service. Figures 6.1, 6.2, and 6.3 compare the Minnesota organizational structure of concentric circles to the actual and aspirational flow charts of a nonprofit group in this study.

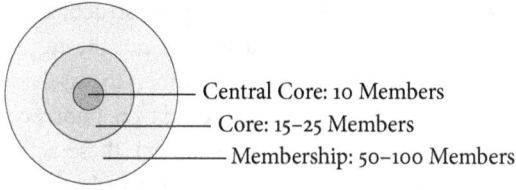

Central Core: 10 Members
Core: 15–25 Members
Membership: 50–100 Members

6.1 Organizational Structure, Minnesota

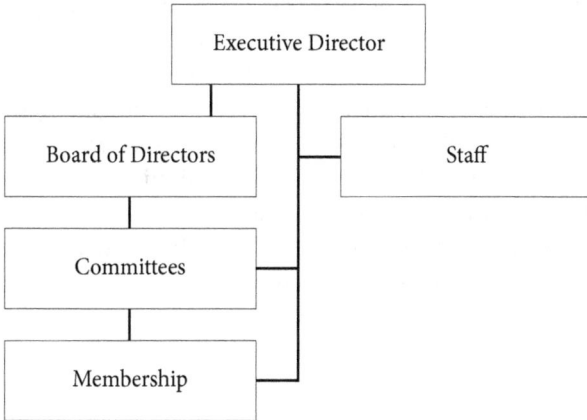

6.2 Common Operating Organizational Structure

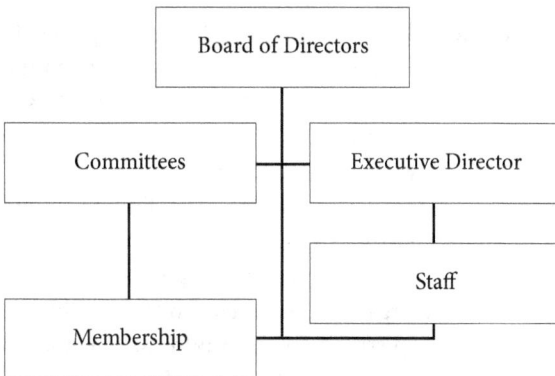

6.3 Common Aspirational Organizational Structure

All the members interviewed felt that this type of structure was one of the key strengths of the organization, in that it truly put the responsibility for decision-making in the hands of low-income women themselves rather than allies. Much like Piven and Cloward's classic text on poor people's movements[5] (explored in a latter portion of this chapter), these activists felt that professional, paid organizers, regardless of intention or background, sapped the potential of low-income activists and directed the organization based on their own perspectives rather than those of the members. This question of the value of paid staff simply did not arise in any other organization; it was assumed as a necessary goal, similar to the assumptions made about the inherently beneficial nature of additional monetary resources.

As the traditional nonprofit models—formal versus actual operating structure—of board/executive director in figures 6.2 and 6.3 suggest, the ability to sustain staff capacity—or grow staff capacity—becomes a central goal of the organization. While this may advance organizational goals if the group is motivated primarily by a service orientation, it is less clear what the impact of this drive for money to sustain staff has on political change movements. Although scholars have explored the impact of professionalization on social movements,[6] there has been little research about the impact of this type of structure on organizations involving low-income women of color and White women.

As the concentric model of the Minnesota organization suggests (figure 6.1), the line between formal "leader" and "member" is blurred. Unlike many of the interviews at other organizations, members/leaders of this group did not constantly refer to one of the "named" leaders of the organization as a reference point for power or information. In other words, if I asked a more technical question about funding, legislation, or policy, these activists did not refer me to the "expert" in the organization (often the executive director). Instead, they generally spoke in terms of the group as a whole. As Belinda Robnett notes in her analysis of the civil rights movement organizational power structure, women who occupied titled positions were sometimes less powerful than those who did not.[7] This finding comports with a general trend in the interviews for this study: titled positions—especially formal board of directors positions—did not necessarily translate into decision-making power within the organization. Thus it becomes difficult to disentangle formalized leadership structures from informal channels of decision making. From the perspective of the activists in Minnesota, this concentric-circle model, without permanent staff, is what sets them apart from the other organizations in the movement.

Political Ideology

Perhaps this pattern of framing simply emerges from the political orientation of the organizations in this study? Recent research on "organizational ideologies" examines the expressive side of organizational structure. SMOs construct frames based on their organizing ideologies, which comprise "core norms, values, and beliefs" rather than solely on instrumental calculations.[8] In their work on the contemporary welfare rights movement, Ellen Reese and Garnett Newcombe posit that welfare rights groups with more "flexible" or instrumental organizing ideologies, such as workers' rights, will experience better success and survival rates than those that adhere to more "rigid" organizing ideologies, such as feminist framings of mother's rights.[9] But I argue that this continuum of political organizing ideologies is somewhat misleading in the context of the current study. As noted in chapter 2, a "feminist framing," if it is used in a gendered colorblindness framework, is hardly racially progressive. It obscures one form of marginalization by layering it over another; in other words, it ignores the inherently intersectional nature of marginalization processes.

Generally, there is little correlation between the "radical" politics of these organizations and their use of particular types of frames. One reason for this is that asking individuals to conceptualize their *own* views of the organizational goals of their organization produces a diversity of responses in terms of scope and tone. It is worth examining these perspectives in depth. Four responses from the Minnesota organization to the question "Tell me in your own words what you think are the goals of your group," highlight this diversity of viewpoint within one organization:

JANICE: I think the goals of the [organization] is that you know *we want to end poverty, you know. It's a big goal. . . . Goals would be to end poverty.* We feel like, you know, end poverty and having affordable childcare, universal healthcare, and a living wage job is what needs to be in place before there can be an end to poverty, and without those in place welfare needs to be there.

LAURIE: Well, *we want to stop the war on the poor. We want to tax the rich. We just think that there needs to be fairness.* You know, there needs to be really, I think there needs to be limitations on how much certain people can earn. I mean like you have your actors, your basketball players, your football players, and they earn way too much money. And then people that work really hard every day.

Like people that are on minimum wage—I mean, I'm sorry, but you can't pay your rent and your bills, your car insurance, gas for your car, all the things that you need to run a household on minimum wage. It doesn't happen. There's a lot of people that have to work for minimum wage and so what's happening is a lot of these people that are working for like minimum wage are working like two jobs, they're partnering up with another person that's working one or two jobs just so they can manage, you know. So, our goal is to, I think, in the future, eventually try to, you know, get people to realize that, you know, there needs to be a cost of living increase as far as the wage that people are earning. The grants, the welfare grants need to be increased—I mean what's the point in having welfare if a person can't have a roof over their head? It doesn't make any sense, like, a household of a parent and a child is $437 a month. Well, I'm sorry, but there's nowhere, there is nowhere in the state of Minnesota that you can get an apartment for that amount. *So, all these people are homeless or they're living with somebody else and I was always under the impression that welfare was a safety net for people, you know, so that they could provide a home for their children. You know, and not have to live on the streets or struggle so much, so we would like to see the grants increase. We want immigrants to be treated fairly.* We, we would like to see the time limit for welfare to—'cause there's a five-year time limit—I think that needs to be eliminated. That really bothers me because I know people just panic when their time limit comes up. And some of these people's kids aren't even in school. And I think a woman has a right to stay home with her child at least until they enter school if they so choose, you know what I mean? I mean why should they have to have somebody else babysit their children, you know, when they can take better care of their child themselves. You know, plus there's a lot of abuse that goes on with other people watching your children. I mean it doesn't happen all the time, but I know that it happens enough for there to be a red flag about that. They've also proven that since these cuts went into effect that the infant mortality rate has skyrocketed, literally skyrocketed because what's happening is these women were not being given any money for childcare, or didn't fit within how much money you could earn—maybe they're making a dollar over or whatever so they didn't qualify for childcare—so some of these women were having their boyfriends babysit their infants, and these men couldn't handle the crying or whatever and are killing these babies. There's already eleven that I know of that's happened since those cuts. Yeah, and those are the ones that are just, you know, reported—we don't have all the, yeah, the statistics for it. Yeah, so, but, yeah, we want there to be fairness, we want the—we don't want people to have to pay co-pays for their prescriptions or for their doctor's visits because a lot of times when people are on welfare or disability, and they say especially people that don't have subsidized housing—all your money is going to all your bills and your rent. You don't have any money left. There isn't any money, so people are not going to the doctor when they're sick, they're not getting all of the medications or any of their medications, you know, that's not fair. It just seems like, there's just a lot of unfairness. *It just seems like the rich keep gettin' richer and poor keep gettin' poorer and there has to be a balance. People should be able to enjoy their lives.* They shouldn't have to struggle and become so stressed out because another thing that creates, I'm sure, troubles in marriages, abuse, and everything else because people are so stressed out they can't deal, you know. *So it's just critical that things change, you know, and so we're just gonna we're gonna battle and we're gonna fight until you know, we see a change. We're not gonna give in. [The organization] does not give in to any, I mean we . . . we come out swingin'—let me put it that way.*

ROBIN: Well one is education. 'Cause most people don't get the information that they need in the low-income communities, especially 'round, like, welfare, know-your-rights kind of thing. And, also to tell people what's goin' on at the state and federal levels of the attacks on welfare. *It also, the other big goal is to empower women to be not only politically active but to kind of come together as a group of people to organize and see that we do have strength in numbers. 'Cause a lot of people [hear] through the propaganda machine that it's their fault that they're poor, but [it's] not, so we want to bring together to know that everyone's in the same boat and we do have a common goal as to not only help us—we don't want to just survive, we just want to thrive also.*

AYANA: To make sure that these programs are in place because *we know that there's never going to be enough jobs for everybody so there has to be a safety net.* And a safety net that should be in place should be one that should take care of a living space for the family that is decent and affordable, making sure the kids have food, access to good education, and for people who can leave the home and work, jobs that do pay a livable wage. Health care. *And those are the goals we're tryin' to deal with, keep in place by, you know, if not, you know, asking for more, but sometimes just stopping attacks just so they don't cut that much.*

While the tone of these responses—especially between Ayana and Laurie—is quite different, all link welfare to broader policy, psychological, and structural issues. Although the Minnesota organization is perhaps the most confrontational in terms of its political rhetoric, this correlation appears flawed once I examine interview discourse in comparison with "official" messages produced by these organizations. This is partially due to the difficulty of separating the rhetoric of the organizations and the actions they take. Moreover, if "radical" is simply a euphemism for protest activity, this is also problematic given what McCarthy and McPhail term the "institutionalization of protest" in the United States: "Citizen protest has now become a normal part of the political process, its messages seen as a legitimate supplement to voting, petitioning, and lobbying efforts to influence government policy and practice. At the same time, the recurring behavioral repertoires of both protesters and police, and their interactions with one another, have become institutionalized and therefore routinized, predictable, and, perhaps as a result, of diminishing impact."[10] Even if we do consider protest to still be the most disruptive form of political action available—depending on how it is structured—any *nonprofit* organization will still have its hands tied due to various legal and tax code restrictions. Typical questions these organizations might ask themselves when considering protest activities include the following:

Why do we apply for a police permit to protest the police?
. . . Because if we break the law, our board is liable.
Why can't we lobby?
. . . Because that would violate our 503(c)(3) status and the conditions of our grant.
Why not just take the streets?
. . . Because insurance doesn't cover it.[11]

It may also be due to the fact that, as noted in chapter 5, race and class politics—particularly race politics—do not map well onto conventional understandings of a liberal-conservative or even radical-reform perspectives. Further, the activities individuals engage in are inextricably linked with

geographical and cultural context that particular actions are not easily clas-
sifiable as more "radical" than others.[12] Some organizations do, however, have
a more conciliatory stance toward "the system" than others. The Montana
organization, for example, generally adopts a cooperative orientation toward
social service institutions in their area:

ROSE: Well, you've kind of answered this question: how are you trying to
         achieve these goals aims—sort of what you see as your organizing
         model. So you said direct advocacy—are there other components to
         that as well, or . . .

NICOLE: Well, if we only did, relied on direct advocacy to organize then we
         would have a smaller group. So, one of the things I love to do—I
         love to door-to-door. I'm totally comfortably with that.

ROSE: It's nice that you're able to do that here.

NICOLE: Yeah.

ROSE: Hard to do it in Seattle.

NICOLE: Well, and right next door is one of the housing projects—right
         next door.

ROSE: I noticed that when I came up.

NICOLE: There's another one right over here. They're mixed in [the city] so
         there's not a specific neighborhood.

ROSE: Oh, OK, so Section 8 is all over.

NICOLE: It is. And so, I like to do the—I like to take the time to just lis-
         ten to people. So many people have—like I was telling somebody
         this yesterday—I have met the salt of the earth. When you go into
         someone's home and sit down and they open up—it's just amazing
         the stories they tell. And the trust level is a little better than—I mean
         it's got be one-on-one. I guess that's what I'm trying to say. I think it's
         important in organizing in this, with this population to meet people
         one-on-one on their own turf. And so I also hang out at the shelter—
         just go there for their family meetings—they have family meetings
         once a week. So, I go and attend. I don't really have a—I just say who
         I am and they know me and then go sit out—and Jeanine [other
         organizer] does this too—go sit out back and just visit and. . . . it's
         also important to have a presence at the welfare office. . . .

ROSE: Yeah, that's interesting. How do you guys do that?

NICOLE: Well, first off by *having a relationship with the caseworkers so that
         they will refer—'cause they see people on the front line five days a*

week. So having a good relationship with the caseworkers so then when they're trying to troubleshoot they'll hand them a pamphlet and say, "Why don't you call [their welfare rights organization]?" And then they take themselves out of it and caseworkers have said: "Can you come to this next meeting with this family? You know it'd be nice to have you here."

ROSE: They actually request for you to come?!

NICOLE: Uh huh.

ROSE: Wow. This is all so new and so different. OK.

NICOLE: It is really different and when we—Montana is so little. [The city] is little, but the whole damn state is little.

ROSE: Right. [laughs]

NICOLE: It is—I mean it—you can get something together really quick here. It's little, but it's good. I think it's easier to organize in Montana than it is in bigger places because we, number one—you can, we've done some confrontational stuff, but it's not, that's not our main focus. *Our main focus is to try to, to have a relationship with somebody so that you can walk into a meeting and not be a threat to the case- worker, but they look at it is as, "Oh," kind of relieved. Or the cops that work the public housing route—we have a good relationship with them and they love it when we come to meetings because . . . well, I don't know that they all love it, [laughs] but this one, but they said that it really helps to deescalate when a family has somebody there.*

Again, this orientation may be attributed to the particular political-geo- graphical (and perhaps racial) context. This organization's orientation was generally one in which they sought to enter coalitional politics, given the tight-knit nature of politics in the state. Indeed, they view coalitional politics as indispensible to achieving their policy goals:

ROSE: We touched on this a little bit, but what's your, what's [your group's] relationship to other organizations that have similar kinds of goals—around social justice?

NICOLE: Well, we do quite a bit of coalition work and without it we couldn't get stuff done the way we do if we were alone. The budget cuts of 2002 were just awful but from that emerged a lot good things, like the tight coalitions. And so we get support from other groups— as far as people of us to give their old computers too—when they hear of funding they send it our way. But we also work strategically with especially, like forward on the next legislative session and in general. And we've worked with, very closely with labor, with the [domestic violence organization], with the choice groups, the [human rights organization]. None of those groups do the work [our organization] does. And, see, that's what's interesting is in Montana—there's not, you know, there's really not, there is [another organization] but that there's not another group quite like [our organization], so it makes it pretty easy to do statewide work. But we work with the churches, some of them, well, most of 'em will work with us to a degree—even the Catholics.

While this group eagerly enters coalitional politics[13] and also cooperates to a greater degree than other organizations with social service authorities, they still rhetorically retain the spark of Piven and Cloward's disruptive politics, as Nicole notes in her description of organizing: "I just, I love organizing low-income people because you're so close to the edge—*you have so little to lose and there's so much spontaneity not—they aren't so calculated—more raw honesty.* And, I think that is just something we don't want to ever lose sight of. And we won't as long as we keep organizing the way we are because that's the voice of [the organization] is people."

This last quote reflects the still "radical" orientation of the organization in some respects, despite some compromises made in working with allies and social service authorities. If we compare this to two activists' responses to questions about coalition work in the Minnesota group, however, we can see a somewhat shared perspective on the poor, yet different orientations toward coalition work and social service institutions:

AYANA: I think the biggest challenges that we face is *other organizations undermining our work.* Or, if we get a lot of stuff done, people takin' credit for it. [laughs] And that's really a challenge because there's been years here that I've seen where we'll, like we had a five-year moratorium and legal aid advocacy project wanted to do a one-year moratorium. [laughs] And it's just like you're undermining our work. If they don't go in there with anything to bargain with, what are we gonna come out with? What do you guys think is gonna happen? *Or they'll tell these people, "Well if you're gonna cut, do softer and gentler cuts."*

ROSE: So, you work with groups like legal aid, but you are kind of also cautious about them?

AYANA: I wouldn't say we necessarily work with them. They work on the same—sometimes they work on the same issues as we do but we don't necessarily work with the legal aid advocacy project lobbyists because we have had issues with the lobbyists in the past before using poor people as a stepping-stone for their career. [laughs] *So based on that we're just really not interested in partnering up with them because they get paid by the state, so they don't want to lose their money either so they're not gonna fight for that much anyways, so . . .*

ROBIN: Well, it depends. The people that work on poverty issues, they're good at coming up with statistics backing up what we always know. And some of them are actually really sympathetic and really like what we're doing. Some of them, I think it has to do what kind of money you get from the government and other—where their money comes from. *If the money is attached somehow to the federal government you're not gonna rock the boat and demand to stop all the cuts 'cause one, you'll be out of a job, and then you won't have any money for your organization. And a lot of the agencies, they just want to, they wanna play nice, talk nice, and then when you do that, you're sort of in a compromised position already.* So and since our money isn't connected to any agencies that have strings or federal funding what we, well, we, one, ask for it all because we deserve it all and we know that our funding, our funders won't be cutting us off. And so we ask for it all because we know if you [don't] ask for it all you're gonna get what the people already compromised to, essentially. So, if you're already starting at a compromised position then you're at risk for losing even more. *And most of those folks who are in those agencies aren't in the same boat as people who are actually being cut off. So they don't really have anything to really lose. They'll still go to work and have a job. And they also don't bring—they don't organize the people.* We organize the people. So they're at the [Minnesota] capitol in their position, but we bring the people to the capitol. For some odd reason that's always a contentious point. [both laugh]

Both Ayana and Robin emphasize continuing experience with poverty as critical to their shared perspective on organizing, which informs their attitudes toward coalitional politics. Nevertheless, this reflects in some part less of an ideological orientation than a combination of political context and organizational structure. Moreover, given the diversity of meanings of radical activity, it is difficult to draw any conclusions about ideological or even oppositional orientation as a mechanism for differences between these organizations in terms of colorblindness frames.

Internal Racial Dynamics

Racial dynamics of leadership in conjunction with organizational structures are the two factors that set apart the group in Minnesota. All the women in the core leadership group were a multiracial combination of either current or former welfare parents; no middle-class, professional women were involved with the daily decision-making processes of the organization. Further, given that there was not just one or two individuals possessing the knowledge, information, and time necessary to make decisions—as is the case in the traditional nonprofit model—there was space for genuine power sharing. In this case, there was real power sharing among low-income women and both women of color and White women. Although this is an elusive fact to pinpoint with documentation, the very fact that every woman interviewed in this organization, regardless of racial identity, had the *same* perspective— albeit using different narratives—about the organization's work in the area of race and welfare politics attests to the power of organizational structures.[14] As women of color in this study were overwhelmingly predisposed to use the race and class consciousness frames, it is difficult to disentangle organizational dynamics in terms of framing in organizations that were made up predominantly of women of color (see appendix C). While this is a critical issue to explore in further research, the central theme of this book is the organizing relationship between women activists across race and class lines. The welfare rights movement is a multiracial movement in which the failure to communicate about race and class threatens the life of any viable national movement for low-income people. In chapter 7, I examine how these race, class, and gender frames affect and reflect the politics of this national coalition and its uncertain future. If internal racial dynamics and organizational structure combine to produce the necessary—but not sufficient—conditions for breaking down this communication and perspective barrier based on colorblindness, this still begs the question of what this type of movement can achieve when these varied perspectives are truly recognized and respected. In other words, what do these internal dynamics tell us about what this movement hopes to achieve, especially in a period of movement abeyance? I take up this question in the next section with the assistance of Piven and Cloward.

Revisiting Piven and Cloward

Over thirty years ago, Frances Fox Piven and Richard A. Cloward penned their classic work on organizing and mobilization, *Poor People's Movements*. As activist-academics, Piven and Cloward's incisive analysis of the success and failure of movements, as well as subsequent scholarship—particularly regarding the welfare rights movement—deserves extended attention in this book. I examine first the importance of this movement in a period of "abeyance,"[15] then engage with the question of understanding movement success in terms of policy outcomes.

The majority of this book focuses on precisely the moments that Piven and Cloward do not concentrate on in their work: periods of movement abeyance. This is a period where the collective disruptive power of the poor is left intact (though immobilized), largely because there is no mass, collective resistance. While the distinction between mobilization and organizing is of critical importance during periods of a mass uprising of the poor,[16] it is still relevant in this context as it directs movement leaders to be wary of the institutionalization of movement organizations after the protests are over. Piven and Cloward's analysis, which pays close attention to critical moments of mobilization of the poor, does not attend to these periods of "in-between" when mass mobilization has waned: "Organizations endure, in short, by abandoning their oppositional politics."[17] Todd Shaw, however, advises otherwise with regard to the contemporary welfare rights movement. He finds that these networks of small organizations are useful not only "to perpetuate and transmit activist networks, protest repertoires, and collective identities,"[18] but also as mechanisms to generate Tarrow's new cycles of contention:[19]

> Whereas disruptive politics are conceivably the power to invoke substantive reforms and social change by fundamentally challenging a political system, diversionary politics are a place-holder politics in that they: (1) lay the groundwork for more effective insurgency (even though a battle has been lost); (2) cushion the marginalized against taking the full brunt of an attack; or (3) create a diversion that buys activists more time. Organized rallies, protests, and press conference by welfare organizers which simply call attention to a grievance may at the moment seem ineffectual. But this form of opposition consistently attempts to push the trajectory of the policy debate at least a little off center at each round and thus incrementally shift its final destination. It is the exertion of this type of insistent pressure—akin to a drop of water chipping away at a rock—for which long-term organizations are intrinsically suited.[20]

While Shaw's water and rock analogy is apt, it still conceives of these social movement organizations as a somewhat monolithic entity. I argue that these organizations still constitute a "movement," even though they are more diverse in terms of goals, strategy, and structure in a period of abeyance than at its crest of mobilization power. It is this diversity of purpose and structure that necessitates not only a closer look at the organizational structure, as this chapter demonstrates, but also the diversity *among* groups of activists (chapters 3, 4, and 5) and their collective identities. Understanding both dynamics is critical to creating a full picture of future movement possibilities. Moreover, attention to policy outcomes in the study of social movements is a necessary intervention; however, I argue that it must be situated within a broader understanding of the multiple goals of social movements, especially during periods of limited visibility.

Piven and Cloward are clearly scholars of politics, yet much of social movement scholarship is still categorized as the study of fundamentally sociological phenomena. While I argue in this book that social movements are always political phenomena, scholars of politics may still be scratching their head, asking themselves this question: what do these movements produce in terms of policy outcomes? Piven's recent work in this area is of particular relevance. She argues that much of the movement literature has remained too closely tied to movement dynamics rather than the ability of movements to affect policy change:

> If movements are regarded as a form of politics, the question of outcomes ought to be crucial, for it is outcomes that ultimately measure the power of the movement, as a number of social movement analysts have indeed recognized. Nevertheless, despite the respect now accorded history from below, and despite some notable efforts to focus specifically on outcomes, work tracing the impact of protest movements on policy remains thin and without much influence on our understanding of American political development. In consequence, schools of thought that privilege other acts, and other forms of power than disruption, still dominate our interpretations of American politics.[21]

Piven's assessment of the sociological character of movement literature rings true; I would also add a general absence of attention to power and how it operates through identity.[22] While Piven's call for scholars to focus on outcomes of disruptive politics and movements is certainly needed, this focus on particular *policy* outcomes is, perhaps, too narrow for scholars of politics.

The central theme of this book has been the ways in which experience, identity, and racial ideologies map onto the politics of a movement that represents groups in multiple marginalized positions. The frames these women use to communicate their stories portend not only the communicative frictions evident within and between these organizations in the movement, but also, I argue, potentially different approaches to the work of social change. While these activists are always concerned with the "politics of survival,"[23] their views on the nature of organizing are more expansive. Perhaps this should be termed the "not in my lifetime" perspective on social change. A Native American woman walfare rights activist from an organization in Spokane, Washington, exemplifies this viewpoint on organizing: "Anytime somethin's going on here, I share it in the community, you know, *plantin' seeds*, you know. And behind all of that it's a lot of fun because we do empower ourselves—it gets your blood going, you know, and it's going to take a long time to see a lot of things turned around, you know, *but and I won't see the changes in my lifetime. But I know my grandchildren or their children will because we've planted the seeds. So we keep pluggin' away.*"

Much like Derrick Bell's permanence of racism thesis, this viewpoint allows activists to take a broader look at the purpose of their work. Indeed, compare the above quote with Bell's famous exchange with Mrs. Biona MacDonald:

The year was 1964. It was a quiet, heat-hushed evening in Harmony, a small black community near the Mississippi Delta. Some Harmony residents, in the face of increasing, white hostility, were organizing to insure the implementation of a court order mandating desegregation of their schools the next September. Walking with Mrs. Biona MacDonald, one of the organizers, up a dusty, unpaved road toward her modest home, I asked where she found the courage to continue working for civil rights in the face of intimidation that included her son losing his job in town, the local bank trying to foreclose on her mortgage, and shots fired through her living room window.

"Derrick," she said slowly, seriously. "I am an old woman. I lives to harass white folks."

You notice, Mrs. MacDonald didn't say she risked everything because she hoped or expected to win out over the whites who, as she well knew, held all the economic and political power, and the guns as well. Rather, she recognized that—powerless as she was—she had and intended to use courage and determination as a weapon, in her words, "to harass white folks." She did not even hint that her harassment would topple whites' well entrenched power. Rather, her goal was defiance and its harassing effect was likely more potent precisely because she placed herself in confrontation with her oppressors with full knowledge of both their power and their willingness to use it.[24]

While Mrs. MacDonald's sentiment is, perhaps, less optimistic than that of the activist from Spokane, their message is the same: we're in this for the duration, whatever that duration may be.

Policy success, in this formulation, is limited and often a means to an end rather than a goal in itself. For example, if a social scientist examined the policy outcome achievements of particular SMOs in the case of the welfare rights movement, many professionalized organizations might rank high in measures of success. In terms of social justice movement building and mobilization, however, I suspect they would rank quite low. This is what we lose when scholars attempt to measure success primarily in terms of policy outcomes. The positive impact of these social movement organizations—those that are not professionalized and have little influence over particular policy choices for the poor—on growing their political communities cannot be measured only though policy outcomes. Instead, we need a more expansive and creative view of what social change entails from a political science perspective. Political scientist Brian Mello makes this point in his study of the ultimate "failure" of the Turkish labor movement: "I argue that a movement's impact is best explained with reference to the type of collective subjectivity that is forged during critical junctures in movement formation. Moreover, I argue that movements that develop what I call alternative collective subjectivities are likely to have more profound impacts in shaping state-society relations than movements that do not. This is the case, I suggest, because movements that develop and sustain alternative collective subjectivities embody identifications, collective action, and a vision for the future that is different from and fundamentally in contradiction to the prevailing state views."[25] At this level, "failed" movements that create or redefine collective subjectivities have the power to make much larger changes than those that pursue and succeed at accomplishing relatively narrow policy outcomes. Welfare rights movement organizations that focus on the larger context of welfare of communities largely fall into this latter category. As evidenced by the earlier responses of those involved in the Minnesota organization, these women are committed to a broader project, while still keeping their eye on daily issues of survival for poor families.

This bias toward lauding movements or organizations that secure incremental policy changes is also reflected in the operation of myriad left-leaning advocacy organizations in Washington, D.C. The level of technical expertise needed to understand federal welfare regulations is daunting; understanding fifty states' welfare policies is a full-time occupation. This has led to a web of advocacy organizations premised on technical knowledge of these policies and how to change them. Two members of such organizations, Deepak Bhargava and Rachel Gragg, publicly called for their colleagues to critically reflect on their strategies of the past twenty years:

> By allowing ourselves to become complicit, by focusing on tiny victories in a tidal wave of bad policies, we delay progressive resurgence. "It could have been worse" is not a compelling public narrative, and few people will be inspired by an agenda that is not quite as bad as the alternative. Every time we trade away principle for a seat at the table, we cheapen all that we stand for. We would be much better off to take the loss in the short term but use it to frame public debate. Losses do have real-world consequences, and it is devastating when more needy people are denied benefits, even at the margin. But we will do far more for our constituencies if we can retake power.[26]

While the tide has apparently turned in favor of more center-left policies with the 2008 presidential election, this challenge still stands, particularly in the absence of any of what Piven terms mass "disruptive" politics by the poor.[27]

Schram's description of Piven and Cloward's long-term strategy as "radical incrementalism"[28] illustrates how this friction between pursuing relatively small policy changes versus large-scale social change is not necessarily a tension that cannot be resolved. In fact, the two may be necessarily connected to one another: "Radical incrementalism challenges the existing constraints on the politically possible, recognizing that the changes forthcoming will be in the form of concessions at best. Yet, such concessions can improve the lives of the oppressed and marginalized and create the conditions for further incremental challenges and improvements in the future. Piven and Cloward's radical incrementalism is a commendable politics of contingency that emphasizes studying the possibilities for action and then exploiting them as best as possible."[29]

If we return to the activist who views her involvement in the context of change over generations—and as someone, who in the quote above, is a "constituent" herself—it is clear that her participation in the movement is not predicated solely, nor even primarily, on policy change. Instead, she is involved in a generative movement. This term reflects Mello's description of alternative subjectivities and builds on it by asserting that movements must be understood as necessarily interconnected across time. In addition, it provides a new way of analyzing social movements that moves us away from the traditional success/failure dichotomy—however it may be conceptualized. Moreover, it allows for a space to consider the contingent, fluid, and interconnected position of movements in the "in-between" moments. Movements, especially in general times of unrest, are hardly discrete entities, either between each other or in terms of what preceded them.

Conclusion

The mechanisms that create conditions favorable to challenging dominant conceptions of race and racism among the organizations included in this study are highly context-dependent. In comparing the Minnesota group with the Washington State organization as well as the six others included in this research, however, two key factors emerge as critical to creating shared race and class consciousness frames among both women of color and White women. Shared multiracial decision-making power, combined with an organizational structure that eschews the common nonprofit constraints, appear to be necessary—though not sufficient—factors in bridging this critical communicative divide. As emphasized elsewhere in this book, these shared frames are imperative in a movement that hopes to challenge dominant views and policies based on triple-intersecting marginalized statuses.

The importance of organizational structure that falls outside of the traditional constraints of nonprofits, both in terms of financial imperatives and the need for a board of directors/executive director dynamic, raises a series of questions about definitions of movement success. If success of a movement or movement organizations is conceived of as primarily a question of policy outcomes, then the goals of movement activists, particularly those involved in ones in abeyance, are only partially understood. I argue that a more expansive view of social movements as generative of broader social change over an *extended period of time* is found in the group built by women in Minnesota. This emphasis should not be misunderstood as dismissive of the need of policy change necessary for the immediate securing of the rights and basic needs of the poor, but rather as an inclusive view of the possibilities of movement or movement organization success. This allows for a refocusing of movement energy on the interconnectedness of issues of race, gender, and economic justice, which necessarily entail a race and class conscious-ness challenge to dominant ideologies of colorblindness. Moreover, in this conception, welfare rights becomes an expansive rather than narrow idea, much like it was in the 1960s. Welfare rights is merely an expression of a deep need for a broader articulation of social justice and the myriad issues that fall under that imprecise but useful term. We will see these communicative issues coming to a flash point in the national movement in the next chapter.

Critical Alliances

Intersecting National Coalitions

> You need to turn off the tape recorder if we're going to discuss
> the national coalition.
>
> —Welfare rights activist

The synergy created by national coalitions offers movement-build-ing opportunities unparalleled in the arena of local activism. This synergy is also fragile and ephemeral. It is particularly vulnerable to the reproduc-tion of broader societal processes of marginalization described in all the pre-ceding chapters. Chapters 3, 4, 5, and 6 explored how contemporary activ-ists navigate the uncertain terrain of marginalization along the axes of race, gender, and class. This final chapter grapples with the implications of these discourses for the contemporary welfare rights struggle as a coherent social movement.[1] One central theme of this book has been the importance of inter-sectional identities and experiences and, to a lesser extent, organizational-geographical influences on the way activists express their views on race and welfare politics. Identifying the frames these activists use is critical not only to understanding the ways they puzzle through the intricacies of identity and its power implications, but also to contemplating how these frames affect interactions between activists and organizations in the movement as a whole. As this movement represents both the real and symbolic consequences of at least three intersecting marginalized identities, the inability or unwillingness to engage with these intersectional dynamics has dire implications for more mainstream social movements.

(Color)Blindness and Consciousness

Since its inception, the welfare rights movement has had to struggle with the complexities of cross-race, cross-gender, and cross-class organizing. The analysis of NOW's emphasis on a particular view of women, work, and independence during the early years of NWRO demonstrates that these challenges were not simply internal: the intersectional dynamics of movement memberships both created and reflected a weak coalition. More important, the policy agenda of NOW reflected in its newsletters indicates a particular conception of women's economic independence and wage work that was largely at odds with NWRO. These contrasting discourses, I argue, reflect an intersectional burden of the welfare rights movement located at the center of marginalized race, class, and gender identities. Although these differing views of women and work may be viewed as parallel, I argue that the absence of a genuine coalition between the two movements partially foreshadowed the limited reach of the welfare rights movement's alternative conceptions of the meaning of work for women, a key discourse absent in the 1990s debate over welfare reform.

These intersectional tensions are manifest within the contemporary welfare rights movement. The preceding interviews with activists across the United States in chapters 3 and 4 demonstrated the central role of the dominant racial ideology of colorblindness in the ways welfare rights activists navigate the difficult racial terrain of welfare politics. Although quite different on the surface, traditional, cosmetic, gendered, and class colorblindness frames all share the same underlying evasion of power dynamics inherent in any discussion of race, whether it is external or internal to the welfare rights organization. These frames are overwhelmingly favored by White women activists, and were found in every organization that had White women members, with the exception of the Minnesota organization. I argue that these frames are antithetical to an intersectional analysis that views race, class, and gender as interlocking identities and systems of oppression. Thus in the erasure of race and racism as a critical centerpiece of all welfare politics, they inadvertently support the reigning racial status quo.

Despite the pervasiveness of colorblindness frames used predominantly by White women activists, interviewees also employed "race and class consciousness" frames that *challenge* the dominant racial ideology of colorblindness. These frames transform intersectionality from a theoretical approach to a practical organizing and political strategy. Race and class consciousness frames eschew a "hierarchy of oppression" approach, embodied in the gendered and class colorblindness frames, which implicitly and explicitly "rank" gender or class marginalization as more important than marginalization based on race. Instead, the women who use these frames articulate an understanding of race and welfare politics in which identity is multiplicative, complex, contextual, and intersectional. In contrast to colorblindness frames, women of color overwhelmingly employed these types of frames when describing their views on race and welfare politics. The few White women who embraced race and class consciousness belonged to a multiracial-led organization in Minnesota. Given this anomaly, an investigation of the organizational dynamics of this group reveals that organizations can play an important role in influencing White women's views on the interlocking nature of oppression, thus reinforcing the sense of shared mission in a multiracial organization. Without this organizational support, however, I argue that White women activists will resort to the easily accessible repertoire of colorblindness frames, thus creating and recreating fissures within movement organizations and, perhaps no less important, between movement organizations at the national level of welfare rights organizing. These frames are critical to understanding the cohesiveness of movements: colorblindness frames both reflect and reinforce existing patterns of political, economic, social, and cultural marginalization in the broader society. In this chapter I explore these framing dynamics in national coalition building, beginning with the emerging challenges facing the contemporary welfare rights movement.

National Coalitions: New Challenges

The collapse of the National Welfare Rights Organization (NWRO) in 1975[2] marked the end of the national mass mobilization of the welfare rights movement. Following the end of NWRO, the movement withdrew into an abeyance process; membership declined but activist networks persisted,[3] ready to be renewed with openings in the political opportunity structures. Although the movement has remained in abeyance since that time, state and local organizations have periodically joined together in national coalitions to organize around federal welfare policy. The dismantling of the federal entitlement to welfare in 1996 spurred the emergence of just such a movement. A number of local groups emerged, which in turn formed regional and national coalitions to fight the new fragmented and decentralized welfare regime. Within the first few years of the twenty-first century, these regional and national groups dissolved for a variety of reasons: internal organizational dynamics, shifts in grant resources, diversion of media attention away from coverage of welfare issues, and the successful campaign to narrow the public conception of "welfare" from a broad notion of economic justice to a narrow entitlement program.[4]

The only welfare-rights-centered national umbrella organization in 2005 (the Welfare Rights Coalition[5]) emerged in 1996 as a coalition of approximately forty grassroots welfare rights groups. Although this umbrella organization was sponsored by an individual welfare rights organization, the steering committee included a number of welfare rights groups from across the country. The WRC was designed to change federal policy after the elimination of the federal entitlement to welfare in 1996, which radically altered the landscape for welfare rights organizers.

This chapter explores how diverging experiential and political intersectionalities map onto national coalition building between some of the welfare rights organizations featured in this book. It is first necessary, however, to outline three underlying challenges in maintaining national coalitions that emerged in the aftermath of the elimination of AFDC.[6] The first of these challenges is rooted in policy dynamics while the second is evident in social movement scholarship. First, the new welfare regime created more than fifty heterogeneous and independent welfare systems,[7] which differ not only at the level of policy mandates but also at the level of implementation. From the vantage point of organizers at the state level, the most useful policy in which to invest dwindling organizational resources is to select state policies that are politically feasible to alter.

This, of course, begs the question of why we need federal social welfare policy in the first place. While those concerned with social justice, particularly racial justice, have looked to the federal government historically for protection from the tyrannical reign of individual state governments, those activists are currently trapped in a bind where the federal government is increasingly *more* punitive and reactionary than some state governments. The federal government sustained this trend with the reauthorization of the TANF program.[8] States have continued to seek ways to carve out exceptions to avoid financial penalties from the federal government for failing to meet caseload reductions. In those states where the state government does adopt more punitive policies than the federal government, however, state welfare rights organizations are left to fight these policies on their own. Despite the recent shift in power at the federal level, the economic crisis faced by states has exacerbated this situation.

The second, policy-oriented challenge to maintaining national coalitions is found in the dilemmas of movement building itself. If the policies that directly affect those experiencing welfare are created and implemented at the state level, welfare rights groups are obliged to attend to these specific needs. Moreover, it is politically risky to focus on national policies if federal officials no longer see welfare as within their political purview, even with the Obama administration in office. As these organizations are dedicated to being the voice for welfare parents, they must attend to these localized needs, especially as their organizational resources are limited. As more parents face their five-year lifetime limit—one of the central features of the new welfare regime—these groups are faced with diminishing grant resources. They must shift their focus, often to more localized problems, or toward current "fads" in the grant-making community such as "civic engagement" projects, in order to survive as viable grassroots organizations.

Finally, contemporary welfare rights groups must contend with pressure to change their organizational focus from "welfare," a term that increasingly connotes a technical and narrowly focused program, to broader issues of poverty. This, of course, is a double-edged sword. On the one hand, this broader perspective allows groups to bridge the artificial rhetorical divide between the "poor" and the "welfare poor," and build a broader movement base. On the other hand, many activists are concerned that the specific needs of the welfare poor, solo mothers and their children, will be lost in the tidal wave of problems currently engulfing working-class families. In particular, attention to the intersection of marginalized identities along the axes of race, gender, and class may be glossed over in attempts to build a viable "unified" movement. Both scenarios reflect unacceptable tradeoffs that are an unfortunate reality in the post-1996 welfare era. The perversity of this moment more than ten years after the elimination of AFDC is poignant: the current welfare regime precipitates the fracturing of a movement just when it is most urgently needed. These fissures are the product not only of the new decentralized welfare regime, but also of larger intersectional forces embedded in welfare politics.

Beyond Welfare Queens?

Chapters 3, 4, and 5 categorized the frames welfare rights activists employ in articulating their views on race and welfare politics. These frames are critical to understanding the underlying forces of movement activity as they signal how movements grapple with images that affect *all* movement members, especially the most marginalized and vulnerable among them. The welfare queen trope perpetuates this process in two ways. First, the welfare queen represents the intersection of triple-marginalized identities along the axes of race, class, and gender. Although stereotypes of the welfare queen are gross misrepresentations of welfare families, including the idea that African American women constitute the majority of welfare parents in this country, the trope is powerful precisely because it singles out one among the most vunerable groups in the United States: low-income, solo, African American mothers. Therefore, this trope stigmatizes all low-income women as welfare queens (thus encouraging them to distance themselves by race privilege or class background), as well as reiterating the stigmatization accompanying marginalized race, class, and gender identities. Second, the perpetuation of the welfare queen image rearticulates the process of secondary marginalization[9] among welfare rights activists themselves. The politics of respectability encourage activists to select the most "sympathetic" (read: privileged) welfare parents as archetypes for their campaigns.

Therefore, those women who have the most privileged identities—in terms of race and class[10]—not only emerge as representatives of the movement, but also, by extension, shape the movement agenda. Therefore, the myriad issues that confront women of color living in poverty, if they are discussed, become "specialized" issues or "additional" items rather than foundational priorities of the movement. Ultimately, I argue that this perspective not only excludes women of color, but also undermines the movement itself by attempting to deny the reality of racism at the center of welfare politics. This viewpoint creates conflict between movement members over agenda priorities and ignores how racism shapes all welfare politics, although the ways women experience this varies based on identity. The former point is embodied by the frames these activists use in discussing race and the politics of welfare. As the preceding chapters demonstrate, women of color and White women offer divergent views on both the politics of race within their organizations as well as the centrality of race in welfare politics as a whole. I now explore how these divergent frames embody and reproduce conflict between organizations attempting to maintain a national movement.

Translating Realities: The Influence of Organizations

Social movement organizations assist activists in translating varied experiences rooted in intersections of marginalized identities into coherent and consistent frames. The patterns in frame usage explored in chapters 3, 4, and 5 implicate racial identity as central to shaping views of race and welfare politics. I posit, however, that these divergent perspectives may be reconfigured into shared frames by an individual organization, as demonstrated by the welfare rights organization based in Minneapolis (chapter 6). But these organizations are quite porous and mutable; it is difficult to analytically disentangle the influence of group members from the influence of institutional factors in creating these shared frames. Nonetheless, these groups do have the ability to bring activists with distinct experiences together, fostering in them the use of common frames. This finding may appear self-evident; it is clear that political organizations are able to influence their membership by providing coherent, shared political messages. But political messages are not synonymous with frames. Political messages are scripts that activists commit to memory; they may be interpretive but lack the depth of an interpretative framework. In contrast, frames are lenses through which activists view myriad social, political, cultural, and economic systems and dynamics. In this respect, they are an integral part of a broader ideological construct.[11]

In the case of race and class consciousness frames, I argue that these frames are not part of a repertoire of frames used by White women activists unless they are at the very heart of organizational culture. In other words, organizations must provide a coherent way that White women can translate their experiences in the welfare system into a broader picture of structural and institutional dynamics; otherwise, these women will revert to the script of colorblindness, the dominant racial ideology. Without this effort on the part of organizations, different experiences with the welfare system will translate into divergent framing choices, which can and do have serious implications for the health of individual organizations. Contrasting experiences based on the intersection of race, gender, and class oppressions, while potentially productive in creating multifaceted organizing strategies, also have the potential to simultaneously reveal and create racial cleavages when building coalitions at the national level, as demonstrated by the decline of the WRC.

Racial Cleavages

In the fall of 2005, I attended the annual conference of the only national welfare rights coalition in existence at that time, the WRC. As a participant-observer and member of one of the active organizations, I am only able to provide a general picture of the dynamics of this meeting out of respect for those involved in this organization. Thirty-five activists attended the meeting, including representatives of organizations from California, Louisiana, Montana, New York, Ohio, Pennsylvania, South Carolina, Tennessee, Texas, Virginia, and Washington State. Even before the activists arrived in Washington, D.C., a great deal of tension had mounted about internal management issues, much of which had racial overtones. The three-day conference included a number of workshops[12] as well as a national action at the Capitol, targeting both the federal government's devastating (non)response to the disaster in New Orleans and a major bill in Congress that included cuts to food stamps and other safety-net programs. Even in designing this action, conflict emerged between groups led by White women who wanted to highlight the legislation before Congress, while many of the organizations who had African American women in positions of power wished to tackle the immediacy of the New Orleans disaster, which had occurred just two months before.

Mistrust between these organizations remained throughout the conference; one concern voiced by some women of color was the feeling that organizations led by White women were using the national coalition to gain additional grant resources for their own groups. In addition, there was discussion of transitioning the group away from a focus on welfare to broader poverty issues, a question that also had racial overtones. Although there were activists who did not fit neatly into these divisions, it was an inescapable reality of the meeting that race affected every interaction between activists and organizations. As of 2007, the group had become largely inactive due to this conflict between organizations and subsequent loss of financial resources.[13] As of summer 2007, new coalitions were emerging, but they largely reflected these same divisions and remained regional in their influence.

Communication Matters

The frames explored in this book were critical to the preceding observations about the national coalition conference. The only White activist who was able to bridge these racial divisions at the meeting was Gina, featured in chapter 5, the only White activist who used race and class consciousness frames aside from those in the Minnesota welfare rights organization.[14] She was able to use these frames effectively to communicate to the women of color in the group her commitment to racial justice. From my own interactions and observations, none of the other White activists was able to accomplish this. This was particularly important because this was the first time the national meeting included a majority of women of color.[15]

Gina's role as a "bridge" between women of color and White women activists at this meeting and her use of race and class consciousness frames is arguably not a coincidence. When I asked her after the national meeting to reflect on the accuracy of this characterization, she responded that she did not feel aligned with the White activists at the conference, so the term "bridge" may be somewhat misleading. Nevertheless, of the White women at the national conference, she was the only one who had used race and class consciousness frames in articulating the entanglement of race and welfare politics. Although welfare is a complex intersection between race, class, and gender politics, class and gender are both implicit and acknowledged. Race, however, is the proverbial elephant in the room in *any* conversation about welfare. It is this implicit presence that demands acknowledgement from welfare rights activists if they hope to truly challenge the current welfare regime. Therefore, White activists who ignore or minimize the racial under-currents of all welfare policy risk both alienating movement women of color (particularly African American women) as well as creating policy changes that, at best, may ignore the interests of women of color and, at worst, may be inimical to these interests and perspectives. The use of colorblindness frames tacitly accepts the dominant racial ideology and the implications of this ideology for existing structures of domination. It also ignores how processes of marginalization based on a single identity reinforce marginalization embedded in other identities.

Finally, the use of colorblindness frames by White activists who insist on the racial-geographic specificity of their organizing strategies and policy priorities becomes particularly problematic when organizing national coalitions to challenge the current welfare regime. Women of color activists, particularly African American women, have particular experiences that, unlike those of White activists, *do* translate to a national level. This is due to the fact that the *national* trope of the welfare queen is one of a long line of racist stereotypes designed to control Black women both symbolically and in reality. For these activists, racial geography, while important in daily life, matters little in the realm of racial stereotypes. If the image of welfare parents is that of African American women in West Virginia, a poor state whose population is only 3% African American, what difference does racial geography *really* make in welfare politics? Although organizations led by White women in predominantly White areas do have different concerns than those in different geographic locations, organizing on the national level requires the use of this race consciousness frame. The history of welfare as national social policy is self-evident on this point.

Squandered Opportunities

Multiracial partnerships that truly respect the leadership of women of color were never realized by this national coalition. Upon reflection as a participant-observer of this coalition and as a longtime member of one of the groups central to the umbrella organization, I conclude that the conflict both reflected in and generated by the deployment of colorblindness frames by

White women in the coalition ensured the destruction of this organization. Under these conditions, there was only one way the coalition might have survived: the organizations led by women of color would have had to withdraw from leadership roles and declined to challenge or question the priorities of the organizations led by White women. According to some of these activists, this was the status quo before the membership of the coalition had a substantial number of organizations led by women of color. The national gathering was the turning point for these activists who were unwilling to allow the status quo to prevail. The White women activists were either unaware of their own race and resource privilege within the coalition, or unwilling to acknowledge how this privilege affected the leadership and direction of the organization. One of the central characteristics of White privilege is both the need to control and the accompanying blindness to this fact. In the case of welfare politics, I argue that leadership by low-income women of color in a multiracial coalition is necessary, though not sufficient, in order to build a movement that is able to successfully address the triple threat of race, class, and gender marginalization embodied in the welfare system.

In conclusion, the demise of this national coalition, while disheartening for those who support welfare rights and the rights of low-income families more broadly, does offer some points of optimism for future movement building. The first, albeit counterintuitive, point of optimism resides in the minimal financial resource base of organizations. The one organization in this study that offers hope for multiracial organizing based on shared analyses of oppression was also the one with the second smallest annual budget.[16] They attributed much of their success as a low-income-led group to this fact; the drive to build resource capacity is not only often distracting and resource-consuming, but also encourages the involvement of middle-class professionals in the organization and increases the potential to cede organizational priorities to grantors. These are not minor factors in the mediating of political action by the poor. Although it is difficult to see when one is enmeshed in the daily work of these organizations, this relative lack of resources may be a blessing in disguise.

The final point of optimism is that organizations led by women of color, at least in the area of welfare rights, are growing in terms of membership and resource capacity. As evidenced by their refusal to bow to the will of more-powerful White women activists in this national coalition, they are acting collectively to assert their own agendas for the welfare rights movement. The fact that they were able to successfully challenge the position held by these activists who deployed the dominant racial ideology of colorblindness signals this growing strength. I argue that this conflict between individual activists and organizations, while painful, was healthy, inevitable, and necessary. Ultimately, if White women activists come to view their own destinies as inextricably bound with women of color, this movement will remerge as a strong force for the rights of low-income families. If not, the movement will continue on without them.

Appendix A

Interview Protocol

The following list of questions was included in the semi-structured interview protocol. For directors or highly involved individuals, I asked a number of additional questions about budget size and organizational structure, and also probed extensively (when appropriate) about the organization's strategic decision-making process. I also generally deviated from these questions depending on the interviewee: if an individual activist was new to the organization, I omitted some questions, while I probed deeper on other questions if an activist had been involved in the movement for quite some time. As this was a semi-structured interview process, I allowed the conversation to flow in whichever direction seemed fruitful. This was particularly true when interviewees became highly emotional. The average length of each interview was forty-five minutes. Occasionally, I did have joint interviews with activists, but they were always paired with someone of the same race (with the exception of one interview). I was usually able to talk to joint interviewees individually as well.

In addition to oral interview questions, I had most participants complete a post-interview written survey. The survey included questions about the following: (1) position in the organization, (2) gender, (3) race, (4) level of formal education (options to circle), (5) income (range options), and (6) age. Not all the participants completed the entire survey due to the sensitivity of some of these questions.

Protocol for Directors and Highly Involved Members

1. How did you first get involved with [organization]?
2. How long have you been active with [organization]?
3. What do you think are the goals and aims of [organization] in your own words?

4. How do you go about trying to achieve these goals and aims?

5. What do you see as the strengths of your organization?

6. What do you see as the challenges of your organization?

7. If [organization] had more resources, what would you use them for?

8. Do you think state and national legislators are responsive to your organization's demands?

9. What do you think are the two biggest problems facing [state welfare program] families nationwide?

10. What do you think are the two biggest problems facing [state welfare program] families in [state]?

11. How do you think the public views [state welfare program] parents?

12. Describe the image of welfare parents you see in the media in your area. Has it changed at all?

13. What is [your organization's] relationship with the media?

14. Are particular types of media more responsive to your group than others? TV, radio, print . . . ?

15. How does [organization] deal with the racial side of welfare in the media? Does your organization actively confront this image (how?) or do you try to downplay it?

16. Have issues of race affected your organization internally?

17. What is [organization's] relationship to other organizations with similar goals?

Protocol for Active Members

1. How did you first get involved with [organization]?

2. How long have you been active with [organization]?

3. What do you think are the goals and aims of [organization] in your own words?

4. How do you go about trying to achieve these goals and aims?

5. What do you see as the strengths of your organization?

6. What do you see as the challenges of your organization?

7. If [organization] had more resources, what would you use them for?

8. What do you think are the two biggest problems facing [state welfare program] families nationwide?

9. What do you think are the two biggest problems facing [state welfare program] families in [state]?

10. How do you think the public views [state welfare program] parents?

11. Describe the image of welfare parents you see in the media in your area. Has it changed at all?

12. What is [your organization's] relationship with the media?

13. Are particular types of media more responsive to your group than others? TV, radio, print . . . ?

14. How does [organization] deal with the racial side of welfare in the media? Does your organization actively confront this image (how?) or do you try to downplay it?

15. Have issues of race affected your organization internally?

Appendix B

Characteristics of Activists

TABLE B.1. *Welfare Receipt Experience Among Interviewees*

No receipt	11
TANF	13
AFDC	11
Both TANF and AFDC	9
Receipt of AFDC/TANF as a Child	5

TABLE B.2. *Years of Experience with Organizations*

Average Time with Organization	6 years
Range	4 months to 16 years

TABLE B.3. *Age and Income of Activists*

Average Age (30 responses)	39
Range (30 Responses)	18–57
Average Income (36 responses)	less than $24,000
Median Income (36 responses)	less than $20,000

Appendix C

Organizations

TABLE C.1. *Organization Dynamics*[a]

	Budget	Staff	Leadership Composition	Membership Composition
California	$337,178	8	Multiracial	Multiracial
Minnesota	$50,000	0	Multiracial	Multiracial
Montana	$219,727	4	White	White
Tennessee	$97,861	2	African American	Multiracial
Texas	$250	0	African American	African American
Virginia	$99,821	3	Multiracial	Multiracial
Washington	$250,847	3	Multiracial	Multiracial
West Virginia	$54,009	2	White	White

a. All information in this table was gathered from IRS tax returns (2004) and interviews with organization staff and members. Therefore, the date range is approximately the same as the dates of the interviews (2003–2006). All of those interviewed in Tennessee were African American. There were some White American board members.

TABLE C.2. *Geographic Distribution of Interviews*

	Interviews
Midwest (5)	
Minnesota	5
South (18)	
Tennessee	4
Texas	5
Virginia	5
West Virginia	4
West (26)	
California	8
Montana	6
Washington	12

Appendix D

NOW Newsletters

DO IT NOW

1971: March, May, July, October, December
1972: January/February, March, April, June, August, September, December
1973: January, March, April/May, June, July, August, September, October, November, December
1974: Vol. 7, nos. 1–12
1975: Vol. 8, nos. 1–5
1976: Vol. 9, nos. 1–11
1977: Vol. 10, nos. 1–11

NOW ACTS

1968: Vol. 1
1969: Vol. 2, no. 1
1970: Vol. 3, nos. 1, 2, 4
1971: Vol. 4, nos. 2, 3
1972: Vol. 5, no. 1
1973: Vol. 6, no. 1

Notes

1. I capitalize "White" and "Black" in this book for two different reasons. First, I capitalize "Black" out of respect and to be consistent with other racial signifiers such as "Latina." My justification for the capitalization of "White" is quite the opposite. Capitalizing White serves to unmask the invisibility of Whiteness. In other words, leaving White in lowercase reproduces the normalization of Whiteness. Similarly, I want to acknowledge that the terms "people of color" and "women of color" can be highly problematic from a critical race theory perspective, given the erasure of important interracial differences in political and lived experiences under these umbrella terms; however, as the findings of this study indicate crucial differences between White women and women of color, this grouping is analytically useful for the purposes of this book.

The terms "Asian American" and "Native American" are similarly difficult, inherently unrepresentative terms. I use "Asian American" throughout the book because, depending on the context, the term may or may not include Pacific Islanders. As "Native American," "American Indian," and "Alaska Native" are also unsatisfactory terms for indigenous people in the United States (especially as these erase specific affiliations), I use a combination of both "Native American" and "American Indian" throughout the book to refer to indigenous peoples. I also use either term when individuals use that term to self-identify.

2. Although the term "welfare queen" should always metaphorically be in scare quotes, the phrase appears without them in the remainder of this book.

3. Cohen 1999, 13; emphasis added.

4. Guinier and Torres 2002, 11.

5. "Social movement organizations" is used interchangeably with the terms "organization" and "group" in this book. I do distinguish between movement organizations and the movement, although in times of abeyance, individual organizations are of heightened analytical importance.

6. See Cohen 1999, 2001; García Bedolla 2007; Hancock 2004, 2007; Jordan-Zachary 2007; Simien 2007; Strolovitch 2007; White 2007.

7. See Crenshaw 1988, 1991a, 1991b; Roberts 1994, 1995, 1997; Wing 1997, 2000.

8. Bonilla-Silva (2006).

9. The works in this area regarding the 1990s debate and its precursors are too numerous to include an exhaustive list. Notable examples include Gordon 1994b; Lieberman 1998; Mink 1998b; Neubeck and Cazenave 2001; Piven and Cloward 1971; Quadagno 1994; Roberts 1997; Skocpol 1992; Swank 2005.

10. Gilens 2003.

11. Ibid., 126–27.

12. Clawson and Trice 2000, 62; see also Entman and Rojecki 2000.

13. Hancock 2000, 2004.

14. Avery and Peffley 2003.

15. Entman and Rojecki 2000; Gilens 1999.

16. Gilliam 1999, 51.

17. Ibid., 52.

18. Lubiano 1992; Neubeck and Cazenave 2001; Roberts 1997.

19. Hancock 2000, 2004.

20. Davis 1996; Kornbluh 1998; Nadasen 2002.

21. Mink 1998b; Shaw 2002.

22. Schram 2003.

23. Gamson 1995; Stryker, Owens, and White 2000.

24. Hunt et al. 1994.

25. Benford 1993.

26. Carragee and Roefs 2004.

27. Portions of this paragraph are excerpted from Ernst 2009.

28. Benford and Snow 2000.

29. Bonilla-Silva 2006, 10.

30. Ibid., 2.

31. Sexuality is undoubtedly a central element of any discussion of welfare politics, though it is beyond the scope of my data collection to integrate this into the book in an adequate fashion.

32. Bonilla-Silva 2006; Frankenberg 1993.

33. Crenshaw 1991a, 1991b.

34. Harris 1990.

35. Crenshaw 1991b, 1251–52.

36. Cohen 1999, 62. I use the terms "marginalization" and "oppression" interchangeably throughout this book. I prefer the term marginalization, as it is more precise in describing the sociopolitical dynamics described in this project. It also emphasizes the active, not static, dynamics of this process.

37. Although this policing is largely symbolic, its consequences are real for those subject to this practice (i.e., Cohen's analysis of external and internal pressures on African American communities during the AIDS crisis). Cohen also asserts that the trope of the welfare queen presents many of the same issues that confronted communities in the AIDS crisis.

38. Cohen 1999, 14.

39. Asserting welfare receipt as an identity is a rather tenuous proposition. The following attempt to assert some form of identity construction should not be construed as an attempt to equate this with marginalized identities around race, class, gender, or sexuality. I want to suggest, however, that it is similar in some ways to class identity, in that it is a somewhat-mutable characteristic (not that gender is not, but to recognize that there is a continuum of mutability). Welfare receipt might be conceptualized as an identity in that dominant society labels this group with a highly specific racialized, gendered, and classed image that recipients have virtually no control over changing. Although Temporary Assistance for Needy Families (TANF) receipt cuts across racial lines, I suggest that the dominant public image of this classification presents similar problems

to that of Cohen's description of secondary marginalization. Although a group itself is highly diverse, the marginalized group has a stereotype that blends all members into a few select images. Therefore, there is a struggle to eliminate the stigmatization of other axes of marginalization from the presentation of that group to dominant society. One might argue that a similar process occurs in the case of welfare: White women, formally educated women, men, who all receive TANF, attempt to distance themselves from the image that contains multiple categories of marginalized identities.

40. Strolovitch 2007.

41. The question of strategic/instrumental motivations of individual activists' use of particular frames is explored in later chapters. From an intersectional perspective, however, this question is largely irrelevant. As I explain in chapter 7, the failure of communication spurred by the use of colorblindness frames creates fissures in the movement itself. Strategically, it is difficult to argue that a colorblind approach has any strategic advantage if it threatens to divide the movement.

42. Strolovitch 2007, 23.

43. Conover 1988.

44. Freeman 1975.

45. *Do It NOW* and *NOW Acts*. Newsletters available from archives begin in 1968.

46. This book cannot make any claims about the attention to intersectional politics by other progressive social movements. There may be examples of movements that successfully center their politics in this way; however, the focus of this book is on one movement that, given its position at the crossroads of three marginalized identities, *should* attend to these dynamics.

47. I arrived at this number through an analysis of the groups included in the Low Income Networking and Communications Project web database (http://www.lincproject. org/), as well as through personal contacts and extensive web searching (2006).

48. Although all these organizations have policy-change goals as part of their mission, they also incorporate a number of other activities as well. Many of these other activities are geared toward education, engagement, peer support, and development of systemic political consciousness. I do not attempt to measure the "success" (traditionally defined as policy-change outcomes) of either these organizations or the movement itself in this research. First, this is due to the fact that the nature of political opportunities for these groups is extremely limited at this point in time. Second, I contest the definition of success narrowly defined as policy-change outcomes. Instead, the focus here is on the possibility that movement success must be defined broadly to include long-term movement building within and between allied social movements, increased community political engagement, as well as policy change (see chapter 6 and 7).

These groups are selected based on state-level characteristics for the following reasons: Most welfare rights groups represent an entire state, not just the particular area in which they are located. Therefore, they must consider all the relevant demographic characteristics of the general statewide population as well as the TANF caseload. Further, while it may be initially tempting to select based on metropolitan area rather than state, these groups must represent the entire state when lobbying the legislature. Additionally, these groups have members from across the state, who may reflect that state's demographic diversity (or lack thereof).

I do not include the names of the organizations or members (including interviewees) of the organizations in this book to protect their anonymity. This is necessary in order to avoid any potentially negative publicity or adverse impact on the funding of these organizations. I use pseudonyms throughout the book to refer to individual members of organizations or interviewees.

49. The cities in which I conducted interviews are the following: Oakland, California; Minneapolis, Minnesota; Helena, Montana; Knoxville, Tennessee; Houston, Texas; Clinch, Virginia; Seattle, and Olympia, Washington; Charleston, West Virginia. I conducted interviews with an organization in Spokane, Washington, but it was not included as one of those in this analysis because it was not a statewide advocacy organization. I was also a participant-observer at the 2005 annual meeting of these groups included in the study in Washington, D.C. Other organizations, not part of this study, also attended the annual meeting.

50. The racial demographics of the TANF caseload nationwide in 2003 were the following: 24.8% Hispanic (of any race), 31.8% White American, 38.0% African American, 1.5% Native American, and 2.0% Asian American (Office of Family Assistance 2004).

51. Soss 2002.

52. Katzenstein 1998, 17.

53. Ibid., 17.

54. Bonilla-Silva 2006, 26.

55. Ibid.

56. Ibid., 26.

57. Using Bonilla-Silva's framework of frame analysis for colorblindness as a starting point, I inductively code interviews to search for discourse patterns. These patterns are explored in chapters 3, 4, and 5.

58. All interviews in this book are transcribed (except where noted) exactly as recorded, though I did eliminate "ums" or other filler words for clarity. I do note places of laughter, as this is an important dynamic in understanding the tone of the interview responses.

59. Simpson 1998, 163.

60. The term "ally" refers to those who have never experienced welfare. This distinction is important (yet sometimes vague) to a movement based on the leadership of families that have experienced welfare.

CHAPTER 2

1. References to the "women's movement" in this chapter refer to the "mainstream" second-wave women's movement. Although I chose NOW as a representative peak organization of this movement, I do not deny the multiplicity of perspectives, aspirations, and backgrounds of various organizations and individuals within this movement. My goal in this chapter is not to emphasize the racism and classism of this organization and its membership, but rather to make an analytical point about the pitfalls of ignoring intersectionality, both in constructing policy agendas of a social movement and in building coalitions between movements.

2. I use the term "strategic" in this book to refer to instrumental decisions that organizers in SMOs must make. This term does not assume or assert a rational-choice perspective about the behavior of movement activists.

3. Freeman 1975.

4. Benford and Snow 2000; Robnett 1997; Snow et al. 1986.

5. Benford and Snow 2000, 625.

6. Castells 1997; Darnovsky, Epstein, and Flacks 1995; Klandermans 2002; Snow and McAdam 2000.

7. Gamson 1995.

8. Shaw 2002.

9. Chappell 2002; Davis 1996; Freeman 1975; Nadasen 2002; Sachs 2001; West 1981.

10. Marisa Chappell (2002) examines the differences between the approaches of NOW and the League of Women Voters to poverty during the 1960s and 1970s. Guida West (1981) also includes a brief analysis of the relationships between NWRO and other women's groups in the 1960s and 1970s.

11. West 1981.

12. Nadasen 2005, 220.

13. hooks 1984.

14. Kornbluh 1998, 72–73.

15. I specifically use the term "narrow" to specify the targeting of a particular group of women's interests (educated, middle-class, White women, in this case) at the exclusion of others, precisely because this targeting is unacknowledged. I argue that the conception of work advocated by NWRO is not merely a pitting of two groups against each other; the consistent adherence to a welfare rights perspective on these issues is broader in that it recognizes the multiple experiences of women across race and class lines, as reflected in the Johnnie Tillmon epigraph to this chapter.

16. Barakso 2004; Freeman 1975.

17. Nadasen 2005; West 1981.

18. West 1981.

19. Costain 1992.

20. West 1981; Nadasen 2005.

21. West 1981, 257.

22. Nadasen 2005, 213.

23. Nadasen 2005, 214.

24. *Do It NOW*, December 1973. These newsletters were published somewhat sporadically, so the volume and issue numbers are not always consistent from year to year. In addition, the *NOW Acts* newsletter publishing dates occasionally overlapped with the *Do It NOW* publication.

25. West 1981, 259.

26. *Do It NOW*, 1977, vol. 10, no. 2, 3.

27. National Organization for Women, 1968.

28. Ibid.

29. Employment discrimination was narrowly defined as specific to the demands outlined in the 1968 Bill of Rights. For example, issues such as affirmative action were not included as employment-discrimination sentences unless they made some other specific reference to government protections (or lack thereof) against discrimination.

30. The overwhelming majority of references to reproductive rights focused on the issue of abortion. I did include a separate category titled "poverty/abortion" to include attention to issues such as Medicaid funding for abortions.

31. Hancock 2004.

32. *Do It NOW*, 1974, vol. 7, nos. 1, 6.

33. The category of "race" was constructed as broadly as possible so as to give the most expansive view of the attention this issue received in the newsletters. Any mention of race, racism, White, Black, and so forth was coded as a "race" sentence.

34. The median household income in the United States in 1974 was $11,197. The third and fourth fifths of the population's median income (by household) were $11,147 and $16,099, respectively (U.S. Bureau of the Census 2005a).

35. *Do It NOW*; demographic terms in this list are the ones used in the original newsletter.

36. Quoted in Chappell 2002, 155.

37. *Do It NOW*, 1976, vol. 9, no. 9.

38. *Do It NOW*, 1977, vol. 10, no. 2.

39. West 1981, 260. There is a remarkable attribution dispute about this quote. Guida West and the NOW newsletters credit this quote to Tillmon. A cursory Google search, however, reveals that it is most commonly thought that Gloria Steinem penned this phrase, although it is phrased as "most women" instead of "every woman." See also Goldberg 2003.

40. *Do It NOW*, June 1972.

41. The image of the "welfare queen," developed in the 1960s and 1970s, provided a convenient rhetorical device for politicians to send racially coded messages to the public about what was "wrong" with the United States. She was also particularly useful in that she represented the actual reproduction of White America's various social fears about race, crime, and poverty. It is this very symbolic issue of reproduction of supposed social ills that link the welfare queen to issues of reproductive rights. This issue of symbolic reproduction is matched by concrete policy decisions to control the reproductive lives of welfare parents by "family cap" or "child exclusion" policies popular in the 1990s.

42. *NOW Acts*, 1973, vol. 6, no. 1.

43. Solinger 2001.

44. Tillmon 2003, 12–13; emphasis added.

45. Roberts 1995.

46. Collins 2000.

47. Roberts 2002.

48. Kearney 2006, 39.

49. *NOW Acts*, 1970, vol. 3, no. 4.

50. "Man-in-the-house" rules, where families were denied welfare if evidence of a man living on the premises was found, were an example of this.

CHAPTER 3

1. Hancock 2000. Although I argue that race is the primary political cleavage in this movement, I posit this relationship within the context of an intersectional analysis. As Hancock (2007) notes, intersectional analyses do not assume that the relationship between identities or marginalization based thereof are of the same significance; they are fluid depending on the particular circumstance (while never losing sight of their interdependence): "For example, while race and gender are commonly analyzed together,

to assume that race and gender play equal roles in all political contexts, or to assume that they are mutually independent variables that can be added together to comprehensively analyze a research question, violates the normative claim of intersectionality that intersections of these categories are more than the sum of their parts" (251).

2. Clawson and Trice 2000; Gilens 2003; Hancock 2004.

3. McDonald and Marston 2005.

4. Bonilla-Silva 2006; Brown et al. 2003.

5. Although I do not wish to wade into the waters over the controversy involving critical Whiteness studies (see Frankenberg 1997), I examine Whiteness for the purpose of naming and interrogating it within the context of gender and class identities. I do not assume a homogenous White identity, and I believe that critical examinations of Whiteness are necessary to understanding the full dynamics of race and racism: "Critical attention to whiteness offers a ground not only for the examination of white selves (who may indeed be white others, depending on the position of the speaker) but also for the excavation of the foundations of all racial and cultural positionings" (1–2).

6. Bonilla-Silva's study of the racial ideology of colorblindness included extensive survey analysis as well as in-depth analysis of 125 interviews (2006, 12–13). Bonilla-Silva's method of parsing interviews about racial issues revealed four different colorblindness frames used by interviewees. Although my interviews are with activists, not "everyday" people, I found that Bonilla-Silva's approach to understanding how people discuss race to be a useful methodological innovation that I employ in this study.

7. Women of color, unlike White women, often used these frames in conjunction with explicitly race-conscious frames (in terms of racial discrimination).

8. Bonilla-Silva 2006, 26.

9. Ibid., 28.

10. This question was asked as a follow-up to my question about race, welfare, and the media. I used the term "racism" only if the interviewee used the term first.

11. Laughter is a common but understudied aspect of what Bonilla-Silva terms the "styles of colorblindness," which "refers to [an ideology's] peculiar linguistic manners and rhetorical strategies" (2006, 53). Frames, rather than styles, are the focus of this book, but it is worth noting that laughter—from nervous to genuine—was a pervasive component of all the interviews I conducted. As an interviewer, I used it to lessen tension, and I suspect that many interviewees did the same. Nevertheless, laughter is a useful communicative tool to minimize or otherwise obfuscate uncomfortable discussion issues during the course of an interview. Displays of emotion are invited in welfare rights organizing, though they are sometimes used as tactics to undermine productive discussion of difficult issues. Sarita Srivastava's work in this area of antiracism and feminist organizing finds that a "'let's talk' approach often deflects and personalizes attempts at organizational change" (2006, 55).

12. All excerpts from the interviews will have sections in italics for added emphasis; Janet is a White activist in Virginia.

13. Bonilla-Silva 2006, 43.

14. As an active member of this organization from 2000 to 2008, I can personally attest to the fact that I never witnessed nor heard of such a training/workshop. Moreover, I conducted a content analysis of board of directors' meeting notes for the period 1993–2003 and newsletters for the period 1992–2003, and I found no references to routine antiracism trainings for the organization.

15. Omi and Winant 1994, 55.

16. Bonilla-Silva 2006, 28.

17. Ibid., 37.

18. Ibid., 41.

19. This pattern is explored in depth through a case study in chapter 5.

20. As I discuss elsewhere in this chapter, colorblindness language may also act as a distancing mechanism for White women who wish to disassociate themselves with the dominant, racialized image of the welfare queen.

21. This is an instrumental choice that organizers make, and one that is certainly not easy given the overwhelmingly negative public image of welfare parents. Of course, this is a privileged dilemma not faced by women of color organizers in the movement.

22. Gilliam 1999.

23. Ibid., 52.

24. Ibid.

25. The racial encoding of the welfare queen stereotype is typically African American, although Latinas have increasingly been subject to this trope as well. I refer to "women of color" organizations in this case because I argue that American Indian women and Asian/Pacific Islander American women also must deal with this image, particularly when one examines the politics of local racial contexts.

26. Rogers 2001, 12.

27. The organization has never conducted antiracism trainings or workshops.

CHAPTER 4

1. Portions of this chapter are excerpted with permission from Ernst 2008.

2. Mettler 1998; Mink 1990.

3. Office of Family Assistance 2003.

4. Frankenberg 1993, 237.

5. While many interviewees often referred to "she" or "her" in response to the question, responses were coded in this frame only if they were referring to women as a group, an identity, or a shared identity.

6. Giddings 1984; Hull, Scott, and Smith 1982.

7. Although this particular perspective is similar to cosmetic colorblindness explored in chapter 3, these frames are more centered on the training of women rather than the notion of cosmetic colorblindness.

8. This extended excerpt follows my first racially "primed" question about how the organization grapples with race, welfare, and the media. Although I recount the individual responses of White women in this organization, it is important to note that my focus here is not on individual attitudes, but rather on the attractiveness of colorblindness as an easily accessible ideology.

9. Gamson 1995; Klandermans 2002.

10. While scholarship establishing coding schemes for the racial content of news media (Gilens 1996; Clawson and Trice 2000) ideally should provide a guiding framework, these previous coding schemes are largely ineffective for this study. Unlike previous studies that search for "hidden" stereotypes in media, I seek evidence that the SMOs in

this study are aware of (and thus not "hiding") the racial stereotypes of TANF parents. Each newsletter article was analyzed for particular words or phrases that signaled race in one form or another. While I had a set list of words and phrases to search for before beginning the process, the process was still inductive in that if I discovered in the texts a clearly racial phrase or word, I added it to the list. Some words, such as "discrimination," were problematic out of context, so they were only included if they referenced racial discrimination.

11. U.S. Bureau of the Census 2006.

12. See table 3.1.

13. Ibid.

14. This information was gathered from IRS documentation and interviews with members of the organizations.

15. The two organizations in Texas and Montana were formed *in response* to the PWRORA in 1996, so I am unable to speculate about the different constraints placed on these organizations before 1996. The organization in Washington State was founded in the mid-1980s.

16. The daily circulation figures for these papers are as follows: *Helena Independent Record*, 13,616 (Lee Enterprises 2009); *Houston Chronicle*, 554,783; *Seattle Times*, 231,051 (Media Management Center 2004) .

17. I borrow David Domke's definition of racial cues: "Racial cues—that is, references by elites and news media to images commonly understood as tied to particular racial or ethnic groups—substantially influence whether citizens' racial cognitions contribute to their political judgments" (2001, 772). See also Mendelberg 2001; Valentino, Hutchings, and White 2002.

18. Search terms included racial identifiers such as White, as well as words or phrases such as race, racial, and racism. The following terms were coded for in all the newspapers: African American/Black, race/racial, racism, White, Caucasian, Latino/Hispanic, Mexican/Puerto Rican/Cuban, Spanish, Native American/American Indian/tribe, Asian American, Vietnamese/Chinese/Japanese, (racial) discrimination. After initial searches for these words, I refined the coding by eliminating references that did not apply. For example, references to "Chinese" in China were not included in the final word count.

19. One White woman in this organization explicitly rejected this frame as well. Her response is explored in further detail in chapter 5.

20. hooks 2000.

21. Ibid.; Leondar-Wright 2005.

22. Oliver and Shapiro 2006.

23. Omi and Winant 1994.

24. Ibid.

25. Kendall 2006, 106.

26. Occasionally, these class colorblindness frames intersected with gendered colorblindness frames, but were coded as such because they minimized or obscured race.

27. Interviewees were not "primed" for a race discussion; I only asked direct questions about race at the end of the interview.

28. This point was culled from other interviews with group members and documentation from the organization itself.

CHAPTER 5

1. Bonilla-Silva 2006, 9.

2. Crenshaw 1991b, 1283.

3. This perspective on legal analysis is not meant as a critique of this method. Rather, I wish to highlight both the possibilities and limits of this type of framework.

4. Crenshaw 1991b, 1246.

5. Frankenberg 1993.

6. In this sense, these types of frames share much in common with representational intersectionality; however, these frames explicitly identify systems, while representational intersectionality includes an identification of stereotypes.

7. The racial demographics of Houston between 2006 and 2008 were as follows: African American: 24.1%, Asian American: 5.3%, Latina/o: 41.9% (of any race), and White American: 53.8% (American Community Survey 2008).

8. Crenshaw 1988, 1991b; Roberts 1995, 1997; Wing 1997.

9. The following excerpt was a response to a question asking interviewees to identify the "challenges" or "weaknesses" they saw in their organizations.

10. All members and leaders of this organization I interviewed were African American, though staff told me that there were White board members.

11. Crenshaw 1991b.

12. A small portion of the interview was conducted together with Janice and Ayana. I did occasionally interview activists together, although it almost always was a short part of the interview.

13. Sexuality, as noted in chapter 1, is a key piece in understanding welfare politics. This issue was of central importance only to the organization in Virginia. Activists implicated sexuality in two ways: discussion of both heterosexism and sexuality in terms of race. First, the group had integrated analysis of heterosexism into their organizing in a way that was not present in any of the other groups in this study. Second, perhaps given the tiny population of African Americans in western Virginia, interracial relationships—and the children of these relationships—continually emerged as a critical subject in the interviews. Although this topic is beyond the scope of this study, sexuality is clearly of critical importance in understanding race and class oppression.

14. Kendall 2006, 91.

CHAPTER 6

1. Berry, Ringquist, Fording, and Hanson 1998.

2. National Governors Association 2008.

3. Hoemann and Baker 2008; Minnesota Legislative Reference Library 2008.

4. "Resources" in the interviews referred to budget size.

5. Piven and Cloward 1977.

6. McCarthy and Zald 1973; McCarthy and Zald 1977; Lofland 1996; McCarthy and McPhail 1998.

7. Robnett 1997.

8. Reese and Newcombe 2003, 295.

9. Ibid.

10. McCarthy and McPhail 1998, 84.

11. Tang 2007, 217.

12. For example, asking women to gather to discuss their lives in rural Appalachia has a different political meaning than it might in an urban area such as Seattle.

13. While the women in this organization generally adopted different forms of color-blindness frames, they did feel as if they were challenging their coalitional partners on racial issues.

14. It is difficult to draw any tentative conclusions about organizations that were composed predominantly of women of color, as White women are not included in the interview sample for these organizations.

15. Taylor 1989, 762.

16. Block 2003, 733.

17. Piven and Cloward 1977, xxi.

18. Shaw 2002, 173.

19. Tarrow 1998.

20. Shaw 2002, 173.

21. Piven 2006, 82–83.

22. Ernst 2009.

23. Schram 2002, 70.

24. Bell 1991, 92.

25. Mello 2006, 2.

26. Bhargava and Gragg 2005.

27. Piven is careful to note in her recent book that a disruptive politics by the poor is not necessarily synonymous with just protest or radical action: "[It] denote[s] the leverage that results from the breakdown of institutionally regulated cooperation" (2006, 21).

28. Schram 2002.

29. Ibid., 51.

CHAPTER 7

1. Portions of this chapter are excerpted with permission from Ernst 2008.

2. West 1981.

3. Shaw 2002.

4. These factors were derived from formal and informal conversations and e-mails with various organization members between 2001 and 2007. It is also based on my own observations as a movement participant during these years. It is difficult to single out any one of these factors given the complexity of these networks and relative lack of documentation of the history of the organizations.

5. At the request of some members of this organization, I have assigned this group a pseudonym, WRC (Welfare Rights Coalition). Given the sensitive nature of the data I collected as a participant-observer in this group (e-mails, meeting notes, individual discussions), my analysis of organizational dynamics is kept at a general level. Some activists I interviewed (after the national conference) asked me not to record our conversations about the WRC. All the groups included in this study are partners in this coalition group; only the Minnesota and West Virginia organizations did not attend the national conference.

6. The legislation that replaced the federal entitlement to welfare (AFDC) with Temporary Assistance for Needy Families (TANF) was titled the Personal Responsibility and Work Opportunity Reconciliation Act (PRWORA).

7. This does not even include separate tribal TANF systems, which present even more difficult organizing challenges given the complexity of program requirements.

8. Deficit Reduction Act of 2005.

9. Cohen 1999.

10. Formal education (as discussed in previous chapters) is sometimes a useful partial proxy for class background.

11. Bonilla-Silva 2006.

12. This included a mandatory antiracism session.

13. Loss of funding was particularly critical to this coalition due to the fact that, on the whole, organizations led by White women had more resources than those led by women of color. If these organizations with a larger resource base decide to not participate, this has a major impact on the ability of the coalition to survive.

14. The Minnesota organization did not attend the national gathering.

15. Before this, the group had been perceived as a coalition of White organizations.

16. The only organization that had fewer resources was the organization in Texas, which had an annual budget of only $250. Its organizational capacity, however, was significantly smaller than every other group in this study. As noted in preceding chapters, in those organizations where I interviewed only women of color (despite the fact that there were White women members of the organization), I am unable to speculate about the promise of multiracial organizing in these specific contexts..

References

Abramovitz, Mimi. 1996. *Under Attack, Fighting Back: Women and Welfare in the United States*. New York: Monthly Review Press.

American Community Survey, U.S. Census Bureau. 2003. "2003 American Community Survey Summary Tables, Custom Tables." Custom Tables. http://factfinder.census.gov/servlet/DatasetMainPageServlet?_program=ACS (accessed December 10, 2008).

———. 2008. "American Community Survey 3-Year Estimates, 2006–2008: Houston." http://factfinder.census.gov/servlet/DatasetMainPageServlet?_program=ACS (accessed December 10, 2008).

Amott, Teresa. 1990. "Black Women and AFDC: Making Entitlement Out of Necessity." In *Women, the State, and Welfare*, edited by Linda Gordon, 280–98. Madison: University of Wisconsin Press.

Avery, James M., and Mark Peffley. 2003. "Race Matters: The Impact of News Coverage of Welfare Reform on Public Opinion." In *Race and the Politics of Welfare Reform*, edited by Sanford F. Schram Joe Soss, and Richard C. Fording, 131–50. Ann Arbor: University of Michigan Press.

Barakso, Maryann. 2004. *Governing NOW: Grassroots Activism in the National Organization for Women*. Ithaca: Cornell University Press.

Bell, Derrick. 1991. "Racism Is Here to Stay: Now What?" *Howard Law Journal* 35, no. 1: 79–93.

———. 1992. *Faces at the Bottom of the Well: The Permanence of Racism*. New York: Basic Books.

Benford, Robert D. 1993. "Frame Disputes Within the Nuclear Disarmament Movement." *Social Forces* 71, no. 3: 677–701.

Benford, Robert D., and David A. Snow. 2000. "Framing Processes and Social Movements: An Overview and Assessment." *Annual Review of Sociology* 26:611–39.

Berry, William D., Evan J. Ringquist, Richard C. Fording, and Russell L. Hanson. 1998. "Measuring Citizen and Government Ideology in the American States, 1960–93." *American Journal of Political Science* 42, no. 1: 327–48.

Bhargava, Deepak, and Rachel Gragg. 2005. "Winning by Losing Well." *American Prospect*, June 19. http://www.prospect.org/cs/articles?article=winning_by_losing_well (accessed November 20, 2008).

Block, Fred. 2003. "Organizing Versus Mobilizing: Poor People's Movements After 25 Years." *Perspectives on Politics* 1, no. 4: 733–35.

Bonilla-Silva, Eduardo. 2006. *Racism Without Racists: Color-Blind Racism and the Persistence of Racial Inequality in the United States*. 2nd ed. Lanham, Md.: Rowman & Littlefield.

Boris, Eileen.. 1998. "Scholarship and Activism: The Case of Welfare Justice." *Feminist Studies* 24, no. 1: 27–31.

Breines, Wini. 1996. "Sixties Stories' Silences: White Feminism, Black Feminism, Black Power." *NWSA Journal* 8, no. 3: 101–21.

Brown, Michael K., Martin Carnoy, Elliott Currie, Troy Duster, David Oppenheimer, Marjorie M. Shultz, and David Wellman. 2003. *Whitewashing Race: The Myth of a Color-Blind Society.* Berkeley and Los Angeles: University of California Press.

Bush, George W. 2006. "President Signs S.1932, Deficit Reduction Act of 2005." February 8. Washington, D.C.: Office of the Press Secretary, White House. http://georgewbush-whitehouse.archives.gov/news/releases/2006/02/20060208-8.html (accessed December 29, 2009).

Bussiere, Elizabeth. 1997. *(Dis)Entitling the Poor: The Warren Court, Welfare Rights, and the American Political Tradition.* University Park: Pennsylvania State University Press.

Cahn, Naomi. 1997. "Representing Race Outside of Explicitly Racialized Contexts." *Michigan Law Review* 95, no. 4: 965–1004.

Carragee, Kevin M., and Wim Roefs. 2004. "The Neglect of Power in Recent Framing Research." *Journal of Communication* 54, no. 2: 214–33.

Castells, Manuel. 1997. *The Power of Identity.* Malden, Mass.: Blackwell.

Chappell, Marisa. 2002. "Rethinking Women's Politics in the 1970s: The League of Women's Voters and the National Organization for Women Confront Poverty." *Journal of Women's History* 13, no. 4: 155–179.

Clawson, Rosalee A., and Rakuya Trice. 2000. "Poverty As We Know It: Media Portrayals of the Poor." *Public Opinion Quarterly* 64, no. 4: 53–64.

Cohen, Cathy J. 1999. *The Boundaries of Blackness: AIDS and the Breakdown of Black Politics.* Chicago: University of Chicago Press.

———. 2001. "Punks, Bulldaggers, and Welfare Queens: The Radical Potential of Queer Politics?" In *Sexual Identities, Queer Politics*, edited by Mark Blasius, 200–228. Princeton: Princeton University Press.

Collins, Patricia Hill. 2000. *Black Feminist Thought: Knowledge, Consciousness, and the Politics of Empowerment.* 2nd ed. New York: Routledge.

Conover, Pamela J. 1988. "The Role of Social Groups in Political Thinking." *British Journal of Political Science* 18, no. 1: 51–76.

Costain, Anne. 1992. *Inviting Women's Rebellion: A Political Interpretation of the Women's Movement.* Baltimore: Johns Hopkins University Press.

Crenshaw, Kimberlé Williams. 1988. "Race, Reform, and Retrenchment: Transformation and Legitimation in Antidiscrimination Law." *Harvard Law Review* 101, no. 7: 1331–87.

———. 1991a. "Demarginalizing the Intersection of Race and Sex: A Black Feminist Critique of Antidiscrimination Doctrine, Feminist Theory, and Antiracist Politics." In *Feminist Legal Theory: Readings in Law and Gender*, edited by Katharine T. Bartlett and Rosanne Kennedy, 57–80. Boulder, Colo.: Westview Press.

———. 1991b. "Mapping the Margins: Intersectionality, Identity Politics, and Violence Against Women of Color." *Stanford Law Review* 43, no. 6: 1241–99.

Cruikshank, Barbara. 1997. "Welfare Queens: Policing by the Numbers." In *Tales of the State: Narrative in Contemporary U.S. Politics and Public Policy*, edited by Sanford Schram and Philip T. Neisser, 113–24. Lanham, Md.: Rowman & Littlefield.

Darnovsky, Marcy, Barbara Epstein, and Richard Flacks, eds. 1995. *Cultural Politics and Social Movements*. Philadelphia: Temple University Press.

Davis, Martha F. 1993. *Brutal Need: Lawyers and the Welfare Rights Movement, 1960–1973*. New Haven: Yale University Press.

———. 1996. "Welfare Rights and Women's Rights in the 1960s." In *Integrating the Sixties: The Origins, Structures, and Legitimacy of Public Policy in a Turbulent Decade*, edited by Brian Balogh, 144–65. University Park: Pennsylvania State University Press.

Domke, David. 2001. "Racial Cues and Political Ideology: An Examination of Associative Priming." *Communication Research* 28, no. 6: 772–88.

Entman, Robert M., and Andrew Rojecki. 2000. *The Black Image in the White Mind: Media and Race in America*. Chicago: University of Chicago Press.

Ernst, Rose. 2007a. "Let's Stay Together: Race, Class, Gender, and the Challenge of Welfare Rights." PhD diss., University of Washington.

———. 2007b. "Move(ments) Beyond Rights: Welfare Rights in an Era of Personal Responsibility." *Studies in Law, Politics, and Society* 40:79–101.

———. 2008. "Localizing the 'Welfare Queen' Ten Years Later: Race, Gender, Place, and Welfare Rights." *Journal of Race, Gender, and Justice* 11, no. 2: 181–207.

———. 2009. "Working Expectations: Frame Diagnosis and the Welfare Rights Movement." *Social Movement Studies* 8, no. 3: 185–201.

Fineman, Martha A. 1995. "Images of Mothers in Poverty Discourse." In *Mothers in Law: Feminist Theory and the Legal Regulation of Motherhood*, edited by Martha A. Fineman and Isabel Karpin, 205–23. New York: Columbia University Press.

Frankenberg, Ruth. 1993. *White Women, Race Matters: The Social Construction of Whiteness*. Minneapolis: University of Minnesota Press.

———. 1997. "Introduction: Local Whitenesses, Localizing Whiteness." In *Displacing Whiteness: Essays in Social and Cultural Criticism*, edited by Ruth Frankenberg, 1–34. Durham: Duke University Press.

Fraser, Nancy, and Linda Gordon. 1994. "A Genealogy of Dependency: Tracing a Keyword of the U.S. Welfare State." *Signs* 19 (Winter): 309–36.

———. 1997. "Decoding 'Dependency': Inscriptions of Power in a Keyword of the U.S. Welfare State." In *Reconstructing Political Theory: Feminist Perspectives*, edited by Mary Lyndon Shanley and Uma Narayan, 25–47. University Park: Pennsylvania State University Press.

Freeman, Jo. 1975. *The Politics of Women's Liberation: A Case Study of an Emerging Social Movement and Its Relation to the Policy Process*. New York: Longman.

Gamson, Joshua. 1995. "Must Identity Movements Self-Destruct? A Queer Dilemma." *Social Problems* 42, no. 3: 390–403.

García Bedolla, Lisa. 2007. "Intersections of Inequality: Understanding Marginalization and Privilege in the Post–Civil Rights Era." *Politics & Gender* 3, no. 2: 232–48.

Giddings, Paula. 1984. *When and Where I Enter: The Impact of Black Women on Race and Sex in America*. New York: Morrow.

Gilens, Martin. 1996. "Race and Poverty in America: Public Misperceptions and the American News Media." *Public Opinion Quarterly* 60, no. 4: 515–41.

———. 1999. *Why Americans Hate Welfare: Race, Media, and the Politics of Antipoverty Policy*. Chicago: University of Chicago Press.

———. 2003. "How the Poor Became Black: The Racialization of American Poverty in the Mass Media." In *Race and the Politics of Welfare Reform*, edited by Sanford F. Schram, Joe Soss, and Richard C. Fording, 101–30. Ann Arbor: University of Michigan Press.

Gilliam, Franklin D. 1999. "The 'Welfare Queen' Experiment." *Nieman Reports* 53, no. 2: 49–52.

Gluck, Sherna Berger, with Maylei Blackwell, Sharon Cotrell, and Karen S. Harper. 1998. "Whose Feminism, Whose History? Reflections on Excavating the History of (the) U.S. Women's Movement." In *Community Activism and Feminist Politics: Organizing Across Race, Class, and Gender*, edited by Nancy Naples, 31–56. New York: Routledge.

Goldberg, Carole. 2003. "Gloria, Hit or Ms.: A Quiz About the Life and Times of Feminist Leader Steinem." *Hartford Courant*, June 2.

Gordon, Linda, ed. 1990. *Women, the State, and Welfare*. Madison: University of Wisconsin Press.

———. 1994. *Pitied But Not Entitled: Single Mothers and the History of Welfare, 1890–1935*. New York: Free Press.

Guinier, Lani, and Gerald Torres. 2002. *The Miner's Canary: Enlisting Race, Resisting Power, Transforming Democracy*. Cambridge: Harvard University Press.

Hancock, Ange-Marie. 2000. "The Public Identity of the 'Welfare Queen' and the Politics of Disgust." PhD diss., University of North Carolina.

———. 2004. *The Politics of Disgust: The Public Identity of the Welfare Queen*. New York: New York University Press.

———. 2007. "Intersectionality as a Normative and Empirical Paradigm." *Politics & Gender* 3, no. 2: 248–54.

Harris, Angela. 1990. "Race and Essentialism in Feminist Legal Theory." *Stanford Law Review* 42, no. 3: 581–616.

Harris, Cheryl. 1993. "Whiteness as Property." *Harvard Law Review* 106, no. 8: 1709–91.

Hoemann, Thomas C., and Barbara Baker. 2008. *State of Washington: Members of the Legislature, 1889–2009*. Olympia, Wash.: Legislative Information Center.

hooks, bell. 1984. *Feminist Theory: From Margin to Center*. Boston: South End Press.

———. 2000. *Where We Stand: Class Matters*. New York: Routledge.

Hull, Gloria T., Patricia Bell Scott, and Barbara Smith. 1982. *All the Women Are White, All the Blacks Are Men, but Some of Us Are Brave: Black Women's Studies*. Old Westbury, N.Y.: Feminist Press.

Hunt, Scott A., Robert D. Benford, and David Snow. "Identity Fields: Framing Processes and the Social Construction of Movement Identities." In *New Social Movements: From Ideology to Identity*, edited by Enrique Laraña, Hank Johnston, and Joseph R. Gusfield, 185–208. Philadelphia: Temple University Press.

James, Joy. 1999. *Shadowboxing: Representations of Black Feminist Politics*. New York: St. Martin's Press.

Jordan-Zachery, Julia S. 2007. "Am I a Black Woman or a Woman Who Is Black? A Few Thoughts on the Meaning of Intersectionality." *Politics & Gender* 3, no. 2: 254–63.

Katzenstein, Mary Fainsod. 1998. *Faithful and Fearless: Moving Feminist Protest Inside the Church and Military*. Princeton: Princeton University Press.

Kearney, Melissa Schettini. 2006. "Intergenerational Mobility for Women and Minorities in the United States." *The Future of Children* 16, no. 2: 37–53.

Kendall, Frances E. 2006. *Understanding White Privilege: Creating Pathways to Authentic Relationships Across Race*. New York: Routledge.

Klandermans, Bert. 2002. "How Group Identification Helps to Overcome the Dilemma of Collective Action." *American Behavioral Scientist* 45, no. 5: 887–900.

Kornbluh, Felicia A. 1998. "The Goals of the National Welfare Rights Movement: Why We Need Them Thirty Years Later." *Feminist Studies* 24, no. 1: 65–78.

Kotz, Nick, and Mary Lynn Kotz. 1977. *A Passion for Equality: George A. Wiley and the Movement.* New York: Norton.

Lee Enterprises. 2009. "Daily Newspapers." http://www.lee.net/newspapers/ (accessed February 1, 2010).

Leondar-Wright, Betsy. 2007. *Class Matters: Cross-Class Alliance Building for Middle-Class Activists.* Gabriola Island, Canada: New Society Publishers.

Lieberman, Robert C. 1998. *Shifting the Color Line: Race and the American Welfare State.* Cambridge: Harvard University Press.

Lofland, John. 1996. *Social Movement Organizations: Guide to Research on Insurgent Realities.* New York: Aldine de Gruyter.

Lubiano, Wahneema. 1992. "Black Ladies, Welfare Queens, and State Minstrels." In *Race-ing Justice, En-gendering Power*, edited by Toni Morrison, 323–63. New York: Pantheon Books.

McCarthy, John D., and Clark McPhail. 1998. "The Institutionalization of Protest in the United States." In *The Social Movement Society: Contentious Politics for a New Century*, edited by David S. Meyer and Sidney G. Tarrow, 83–110. Lanham, Md.: Rowman & Littlefield.

McCarthy, John D., and Mayer N. Zald. 1973. *The Trend of Social Movements in America: Professionalization and Resource Mobilization.* New Brunswick, N.J.: Transaction Publishers.

———. 1977. "Resource Mobilization and Social Movements: A Partial Theory." *American Journal of Sociology* 82, no. 2: 1212–41.

McDonald, Catherine, and Greg Marston. 2005. "Workfare as Welfare: Governing Unemployment in the Advanced Liberal State." *Critical Social Policy* 25, no. 3: 374–401.

Media Management Center. 2004. "Top 50 Newspapers by Circulation, 2004." http://www.mediainfocenter.org/compare/top50/ (accessed February 1, 2010).

Mello, Brian Jason. 2006. "Evaluating Social Movement Impacts: Labor and the Politics of State-Society Relations." PhD diss., University of Washington.

Mendelberg, Tali. 2001. *The Race Card: Campaign Strategy, Implicit Messages, and the Norm of Equality.* Princeton: Princeton University Press.

Mettler, Suzanne. 1998. *Dividing Citizens: Gender and Federalism in New Deal Public Policy.* Ithaca: Cornell University Press.

Mink, Gwendolyn. 1990. "The Lady and the Tramp: Gender, Race, and the Origins of the American Welfare State." In *Women, the State, and Welfare*, edited by Linda Gordon, 92–122. Madison: University of Wisconsin Press.

———. 1998a. "The Lady and the Tramp (II): Feminist Welfare Politics, Poor Single Mothers, and the Challenge of Welfare Justice." *Feminist Studies* 24, no. 1: 55–64.

———. 1998b. *Welfare's End.* Ithaca: Cornell University Press.

Minnesota Legislative Reference Library. 2008. "Party Control of the Minnesota House of Representatives, 1951–Present." http://www.leg.state.mn.us/lrl/histleg/caucush.asp (accessed December 2, 2008).

Moynihan, Daniel Patrick. 2003. "The Negro Family: A Case for National Action." In *Welfare: A Documentary History of U.S. Policy and Politics*, edited by Gwendolyn Mink and Rickie Solinger, 226–39. New York: New York University Press.

Nadasen, Premilla. 2002. "Expanding the Boundaries of the Women's Movement: Black Feminism and the Struggle of Welfare Rights." *Feminist Studies* 28, no. 2: 270–301.

———. 2005. *Welfare Warriors: The Welfare Rights Movement in the United States.* New York: Routledge.

Naples, Nancy A. 1998a. *Grassroots Warriors: Activist Mothering, Community Work, and the War on Poverty.* New York: Routledge.

National Governors Association. "Governors." 2008. http://www.nga.org/ (accessed December 2, 2008).

National Organization for Women. 1968. "Bill of Rights, 1968." Washington, D.C: National Organization for Women. http://coursesa.matrix.msu.edu/hst203/documents/now-rights.html. (accessed September 2, 2007).

Neubeck, Kenneth J., and Noel A. Cazenave. 2001. *Welfare Racism: Playing the Race Card Against America's Poor.* New York: Routledge.

Newman, Louise Michele. 1999. *White Women's Rights: The Racial Origins of Feminism in the United States.* New York: Oxford University Press.

Office of Family Assistance, Administration for Children and Families, U.S. Department of Health and Human Services. 2003. "Temporary Assistance for Needy Families Program (TANF): Fifth Annual Report to Congress." Washington, D.C.: Office of Family Assistance, Administration for Children and Families, U.S. Department of Health and Human Services. http://www.acf.hhs.gov/programs/ofa/data-reports/annualreport5/index.htm (accessed January 31, 2010).

———. 2004. "National TANF Datafile as of 4/15/2003." Washington, D.C.: Office of Family Assistance, Administration for Children and Families, U.S. Department of Health and Human Services. http://www.acf.hhs.gov/programs/ofa/character/FY2003/1008.htm (accessed January 31, 2010).

Oliver, Melvin L., and Thomas M. Shapiro. 2006. *Black Wealth/White Wealth: A New Perspective on Racial Inequality.* New York: Routledge.

Omi, Michael, and Howard Winant. 1994. *Racial Formation in the United States: From the 1960s to the 1990s.* New York: Routledge.

Orleck, Annalise. 1997. "'If It Wasn't For You I'd Have Shoes For My Children': The Political Education of Las Vegas Welfare Mothers." In *The Politics of Motherhood: Activist Voices From Left to Right,* edited by Alexis Jetter, Annelise Orleck, and Diana Taylor, 102–18. Hanover: University Press of New England.

Piven, Frances Fox . 2006. *Challenging Authority: How Ordinary People Change America.* Lanham, Md.: Rowman & Littlefield.

Piven, Frances Fox, and Richard A. Cloward. 1971. *Regulating the Poor: The Functions of Public Welfare.* New York: Vintage Books.

———. 1977. *Poor People's Movements: Why They Succeed, How They Fail.* New York: Vintage Books.

Quadagno, Jill. 1994. *The Color of Welfare: How Racism Undermined the War on Poverty.* New York: Oxford University Press.

Reese, Ellen, and Garnett Newcombe. 2003. "Income Rights, Mothers' Rights, or Workers' Rights? Collective Action Frames, Organizational Ideologies, and the American Welfare Rights Movement." *Social Problems* 50, no. 2: 294–318.

Roberts, Dorothy E. 1994. "The Value of Black Mothers' Work." *Connecticut Law Review* 26 (Spring): 871–78.

———. 1995. "Racism and Patriarchy in the Meaning of Motherhood." In *Mothers in Law: Feminist Theory and the Legal Regulation of Motherhood*, edited by Martha Albertson Fineman and Isabel Karpin, 149–224. New York: Columbia University Press.

———. 1997. *Killing the Black Body: Race, Reproduction, and the Meaning of Liberty*. New York: Vintage Books.

———. 2002. *Shattered Bonds: The Color of Child Welfare*. New York: Basic Books.

Roberts, Paula. 2005. "The Marriage and Fatherhood Provisions of the Deficit Reduction Act of 2005." Washington, D.C.: Center for Law and Social Policy.

Robnett, Belinda. 1997. *How Long? How Long?: African-American Women in the Struggle for Civil Rights*. New York: Oxford University Press.

Rogers, David. 2001. "Diversity Training: Good for Business but Insufficient for Social Change." *Western States Center Views* 21 (Winter): 12–13.

Sachs, Andrea Jule. 2001. "The Politics of Poverty: Race, Class, Motherhood, and the National Welfare Rights Organization, 1965–1975." PhD diss., University of Minnesota.

Schram, Sanford F . 2002. *Praxis for the Poor: Piven and Cloward and the Future of Social Science in Social Welfare*. New York: New York University Press.

———. 2003. "Putting a Black Face on Welfare: The Good and the Bad." In *Race and the Politics of Welfare Reform*, edited by Sanford F. Schram, Joe Soss, and Richard C. Fording, 196–224. Ann Arbor: University of Michigan Press.

Shaw, Todd. 2002. "We Refused to Lay Down Our Spears: The Persistence of Welfare Rights Activism, 1966–1996." In *Black Political Organizations in the Post–Civil Rights Era*, edited by Ollie A. Johnson III and Karin L. Stanford, 170–92. New Brunswick: Rutgers University Press.

Simien, Evelyn M. 2007. "Doing Intersectionality Research: From Conceptual Issues to Practical Examples." *Politics & Gender* 3, no. 2: 264–71.

Simpson, Andrea Y. 1998. *The Tie That Binds: Identity and Political Attitudes in the Post–Civil Rights Generation*. New York: New York University Press.

Skocpol, Theda. 1992. *Protecting Soldiers and Mothers: The Political Origins of Social Policy in the United States*. Cambridge, Mass.: Belknap Press.

Snow, David. A., E. Burke Rochford Jr., Steven K. Worden, and Robert D. Benford. 1986. "Frame Alignment Processes, Micromobilization, and Movement Participation." *American Sociological Review* 51, no. 4: 464–81.

Solinger, Rickie. 2001. *Beggars and Choosers: How the Politics of Choice Shapes Adoption, Abortion, and Welfare in the United States*. New York: Hill and Wang.

Soss, Joe. 2002. "Race and Welfare in the United States: Presentation to the CHN Welfare Advocates Meeting." Conference presentation to CHN Welfare Advocates Meeting, January 15.

Srivastava, Sarita. 2006. "Tears, Fears, and Careers: Anti-racism and Emotion in Social Movement Organizations." *Canadian Journal of Sociology* 31, no. 1: 55–90.

Strolovitch, Dara Z. 2007. *Affirmative Advocacy: Race, Class, and Gender in Interest Group Politics*. Chicago: University of Chicago Press.

Stryker, Sheldon, Timothy J. Owens, and Robert W. White, eds. 2000. *Self, Identity, and Social Movements*. Minneapolis: University of Minnesota Press.

Swank, Duane. 2005. "Globalisation, Domestic Politics, and Welfare State Retrenchment in Capitalist Democracies." *Social Policy and Society* 4, no. 2: 183–95.

Tang, Eric. 2007. "Non-profits and the Autonomous Grassroots." In *The Revolution Will Not Be Funded: Beyond the Non-profit Industrial Complex*, edited by INCITE! Women of Color Against Violence, 215–25. Cambridge, Mass.: South End Press.

Tarrow, Sidney. 1998. *Power in Movement: Social Movements, Collective Action, and Politics.* New York: Cambridge University Press.

———. 2003. "Crossing the Ocean and Back Again with Piven and Cloward." *Perspectives on Politics* 1, no. 4: 711–14.

Taylor, Verta. 1989. "Social Movement Continuity: The Women's Movement in Abeyance." *American Sociological Review* 54, no. 5: 761–75.

Themba-Nixon, Makani. 2000. "The Stories They Tell: Media Coverage of Welfare." *GRIPP News and Notes* 2, no. 1: 4.

Tillmon, Johnnie. 2003. "Welfare Is a Women's Issue." In *Welfare: A Documentary History of U.S. Policy and Politics*, edited by Gwendolyn Mink and Rickie Solinger, 373–79. New York: New York University Press.

U.S. Bureau of the Census. 2004. "Table 4: Annual Estimates of the Population by Race Alone and Hispanic or Latino Origin for the United States and States: July 1, 2003 (SC–EST2003–04)." Washington, D.C.: U.S. Bureau of the Census. http://www.census.gov/popest/states/asrh/SC-EST2004-04.html (accessed December 10, 2008).

———. 2005a. "Historical Income Tables—Households, Table H-3: Mean Household Income Received by Each Fifth and Top 5 Percent All Races: 1967 to 2005." Washington, D.C.: U.S. Bureau of the Census. http://www.census.gov/hhes/www/income/histinc/h03ar.html (accessed December 10, 2008).

———. 2005b. "Historical Income Tables—Households, Table H-5: Race and Hispanic Origin of Householder—Households by Median and Mean Income: 1967 to 2005." Washington, D.C.: U.S. Bureau of the Census. http://www.census.gov/hhes/www/income/histinc/h05.html (accessed December 10, 2008).

———. 2006. "Statistical Abstract of the United States, 2006: Persons Below Poverty Level, 2003." Washington, D.C.: U.S. Bureau of the Census. http://www.census.gov/hhes/www/poverty.html (accessed February 1, 2010).

U.S. Bureau of the Census, Small Area Estimates Branch. 2005. "Table 1: 2003 Poverty and Median Income Estimates." Washington, D.C.: U.S. Bureau of the Census. http://www.census.gov/hhes/www/saipe (accessed December 10, 2008).

Valentino, Nicholas A., Vincent L. Hutchings, and Ismail K. White. 2002. "Cues That Matter: How Political Ads Prime Racial Attitudes During Campaigns." *American Political Science Review* 96, no. 1: 75–90.

Van Dijk, T. 1993. *Elite Discourse and Racism.* Newbury Park, Calif.: Sage Publications.

West, Guida. 1981. *The National Welfare Rights Movement: The Social Protest of Poor Women.* New York: Praeger.

White, Julie Anne. 2007. "The Hollow and the Ghetto: Space, Race, and the Politics of Poverty." *Politics & Gender* 3, no. 2: 271–80.

Wing, Adrien Katherine. 1997. "Introduction." In *Critical Race Feminism: A Reader*, edited by Adrien Katherine Wing, 1–5. New York: New York University Press.

———. 2000. "Introduction." In *Global Critical Race Feminism: An International Reader*, edited by Adrienne Katherine Wing, 1–6. New York: New York University Press.

Young, Iris Marion. 1997. *Intersecting Voices: Dilemmas of Gender, Political Philosophy, and Policy.* Princeton: Princeton University Press.

Index

colorblindness frames, 6–7, 13; organizational culture and, 147; organizational dynamics of, 143; power dynamics and, 142; as racial ideology, 38–39, 63, 169n6; universal humanity and, 41–42; Whiteness as status quo and, 56–57. *See also* class colorblindness; cosmetic colorblindness; gendered colorblindness; traditional colorblindness

colorblindness/power evasiveness, 67

contention, cycles of, 134

cosmetic colorblindness, 38–39, 53–62; as racial ideology, 62–63; *vs.* structural intersectionality, 93–97; White women and, 40

Crenshaw, Kimberlé Williams, 7–8, 93, 101

critical race theory, 93

cross-class organizing, 84

cultural racism, 46

culture, class as, 83

demographics, 60–62; of organizations, 81–82; of states, 73–75, 119t; of TANF caseloads, 12, 48–49t, 166n50

discursive patterns, 13

disruptive politics, 134, 173n27

diversionary politics, 134

Domke, David, 171n17

double oppression, 69

education: and class background, 114; popular, 107–9

employment discrimination, 34, 167n29

ERA (Equal Rights Amendment) in NOW newsletters, 27

essentialist racism, 67

experiential intersectionality, 104–7

Families First, 101. *See also* TANF; welfare

Family Assistance Plan, 27

fathers and welfare, 33–34, 168n50

feminism, critical race, 1–2, 7–8, 69

food stamps, 103–4

Fording, Richard C., 119–20

frames: defined, 6, 13; interviews and, 14; management, 57–58; neutralization, 57–62; *vs.* political messages, 147; welfare rights organizations and, 7. *See also* colorblindness frames; race and class consciousness frames

Frankenberg, Ruth, 7, 67

Gamson, Joshua, 21

gender: collective identity of, 34; and diminishment of race, 68; as metaphor for Whiteness, 82

gendered colorblindness, 66–83; other frames and, 72; secondary marginalization and, 82–83; Washington State organization and, 76; White women and, 68–77; women of color and, 77–83

geographical contexts: gendered colorblindness and, 72; minimization of racism and, 44–45; traditional colorblindness and, 47

Gilens, Martin, 4

Gilliam, Franklin D., 5, 54

Gragg, Rachel, 138

Guinier, Lani, 2

Hancock, Ange-Marie, 4, 5, 27, 168n1

Hanson, Russell L., 119–20

Helena (Montana), 44–45, 75

Helena Independent Record, 75–76, 76t

hierarchies of oppression, 85–87, 110, 142–43

"Housewives and Other Shut-Ins" (NOW article), 30–31

Houston (Texas), 75–76, 96, 109

Houston Chronicle, 75–76, 76t

hyperfertility, stereotype of, 27, 33

identities, multiplicative effects of, 7–10, 21–22, 164n39

income status as class, 66

income *vs.* wealth, 83

influence of social movement organizations, 146–47

institutional racism, 109–10

instrumental neutralization, 58, 59–62

interest groups, single-identity, 8
intersectional burdens, 22; welfare rights movement and, 34–35, 168n1
intersectional frameworks, 21
intersectionality: coalitions and, 34; experiential, 104–7; marginalization and, 91–92, 93; between NOW and NWRO, 82; political, 7–8, 9–10, 93, 97–101; of race and class consciousness frames, 93, 142–43; representational, 101–4, 172n6; and SMOs, 2–3; structural, 93–97; within welfare rights movement, 11–12
intersectional tensions between NOW and NWRO, 142–43
interviews and frames, 14
"It's Not Pop Who Pays" (NOW article), 33–34

Katrina (hurricane), 1, 76, 94, 96–97, 147–48
Kendall, Frances E., 84–85, 110
Kornbluh, Felicia A., 22

labor movements, Turkish, 137
Latinas, 74, 94–95. *See also* women of color
laughter, 169n11
leadership: racial identity and, 10, 37–38; social movement mobilization and, 72–73
liberalism, abstract, 41–43, 45–46

MacDonald, Biona, 136–37
management frames, 57–58
marginalization, 37; anti-oppression trainings, 78–80, 99; of identities, 2, 35; intersecting, 91–92, 93; secondary, 8–9, 10, 82–83, 146, 164n39. *See also* oppression
Marxist approaches to race, 84
McCarthy, John D., 128
McPhail, Clark, 128
media: African American women in, 96–97; power imbalance with social movements, 6; race and welfare in, 111–12; racial stereotypes in, 53–54, 87; relaying messages to, 70; welfare in, 4–5
Mello, Brian, 137, 139

messages: organizational, 73, 170n10; political, 147
Minneapolis/St. Paul (Minnesota), 47, 111, 118
Minnesota compared to Washington, 118–20
Minnesota organization, 47, 120–24, 131–32
Montana, media coverage of poverty in, 74–76
motherhood, 19, 23, 35
Moynihan, Daniel Patrick, 46
multiplicative effects of identities, 7–10, 21–22, 164n39

Nadasen, Premilla, 23
national coalitions, 17, 141, 143–51; challenges in maintaining, 144–45; conference, 148–50; demise of, 150; racial-geographic specificity and, 149
National Organization for Women (NOW). *See* NOW
National Welfare Rights Organization (NWRO). *See* NWRO
Native Americans, 44–45, 56, 60–61, 74. *See also* women of color
naturalization, 46
"The Negro Family: A Case for National Action" (Moynihan), 46
neoliberalism, 41
neutralization frames, 57–62
Newcombe, Garnett, 125
New Orleans (Louisiana), 1. *See also* Katrina
newsletters, NOW: analysis of, 34; child support in, 45; coding of, 24–26; NWRO in, 27–28; poverty and welfare in, 26–27, 29; race in, 28–30, 29t; results of coding, 26–31, 27t, 28t; welfare in, 31
newsletters, Washington State organization, 73, 74t, 170n10
newspapers, analysis of, 11, 73–76, 76t, 171n18
NOW (National Organization for Women), 10–11, 20; "Bill of Rights," 11, 25, 26; child support and, 33; demographics of membership, 29; employment discrimination, 34; newsletters of, 24–31, 34, 45; poor women and, 24; relationship with NWRO, 21, 22, 23–24, 82, 142–43; welfare and work in, 30–33; as White, middle-class organization, 29–30

NWRO (National Welfare Rights Organization), 10–11, 20; abeyance process and, 143; leadership of, 23; marginalized identities and, 35; mentions in NOW newsletters, 27–28; relationship with NOW, 21, 22, 23–24, 82, 142–43; view of work and, 32–33, 167n15

Oakland (California), 52, 107–9
Oliver, Melvin L., 83
Omi, Michael, 84
oppression, 3; anti-oppression trainings, 78–80, 99; double, 69; hierarchies of, 85–87, 110, 142–43; systemic analysis of, 112–14. *See also* marginalization
organizational structures, 120–24; colorblindness and, 47, 118, 143, 147; internal racial dynamics in, 133; operating models of, 123f
organizations: dynamics between, 99–101; dynamics within, 98–99; racial composition of, 81–82; radical orientation of, 131–33; staff capacity of, 121t; women of color organizations, 70–72

Peffley, Mark, 4
Piven, Frances Fox, 117; disruptive politics, 131, 173n27; organizational structure, 124; radical incrementalism, 138; success and failure of social movements, 134–35
policy change, social movements and, 135–39, 165n48
political ideology, 119–20, 125–33
political intersectionality, 7–8, 9–10, 93, 97–101
political landscape of Washington and Minnesota, 119
political messages *vs.* frames, 147
politics, disruptive *vs.* diversionary, 134, 173n27
Poor People's Movements (Piven and Cloward), 117, 134
poverty: as broader issue for welfare rights groups, 145; racialized as African American, 4–5; by state and caseload, 48–49t; welfare as problem of, 83; welfare participation and, 67

poverty coverage in local newspapers, 73–76
power and management frames, 57
power dynamics and colorblindness, 142
power imbalances, 6
privilege, White, 42–43, 78–79, 115, 150. *See also* Whiteness; White women
protest activity, 128
public identity, welfare queen as, 5
public opinion, welfare in, 4–5

queer movements, 21

race: as cosmetic, 60; diminishment of, 68; discrimination and, 106–7; Marxist approach to, 84; organizational messages and, 73, 170n10; by state and caseload, 48–49t; as synonym for "people of color," 59–60; welfare and, 149; and welfare in the media, 111–12; welfare rights movement and, 37
race and class consciousness frames, 91–116, 147, 172n6; intersectionality and, 142–43; at national coalition conference, 148–49; White women and, 111–18; women of color, 92–110
race cognizance, 67
race theory, critical, 93
racial cleavages, 147–49
racial cues in publications, 74t, 76t, 171n17. *See also* newsletters, NOW; newsletters, Washington State organization; newspapers, analysis of
racial demographics, 60–62; of organizations, 81–82; of states, 73–75, 119t; of TANF program, 12
racial diversity *vs.* racial justice, 59–62
racial dynamics, 61, 133
racial geography, 149
racial identity of movement leaders, 37–38
racial ideologies, 6, 13, 91; of colorblindness, 38, 169n6; cosmetic colorblindness and, 62–63. *See also* colorblindness frames
racial justice *vs.* racial diversity, 59–62

"welfare queen" trope: as cross-cutting issue, 8; meaning of work and, 22; NOW newsletters and, 27; perceptions of White *vs.* Black, 53–54; political intersectionality and, 98; as public identity, 5, 168n41; race and, 37; representational intersectionality and, 101–4; welfare rights organizations and, 145–46; women of color organizations and, 58, 149. *See also* stereotypes

Welfare Rights Coalition, 143–44

welfare rights movement, 2, 141–42; construction of frames in, 22; intersectional burden and, 34–35; intersectionality within, 11–12; meaning of "work" by, 9, 22; relationship with women's movement, 10–11; self-definition for, 9

welfare rights organizations: broad issue of poverty and, 145; budgets and, 120–22, 121t, 150; experience of welfare and, 110; frames and, 7; organizing ideologies of, 125

West, Guida, 21, 23

West Virginia, welfare parents in, 61–62

Whiteness: gender as metaphor for, 82; as normalized, 38, 44, 169n5; as status quo, 56–57

White women: class colorblindness and, 85–87; cosmetic colorblindness and, 39; gendered colorblindness and, 68–77; as majority of TANF caseload, 12; privilege and, 42–43, 78–79, 115, 150; race and class consciousness and, 111–18; secondary marginalization and, 10; traditional colorblindness and, 40–47

White Women, Race Matters: The Social Construction of Whiteness (Frankenberg), 7

Wiley, George A., 23

Winant, Howard, 84

womanhood, core of, 68–69

women as strategic bodies, 70, 170n7

women of color: arranging of, 53–54; as caseworkers, 52; class colorblindness and, 88–90; gendered colorblindness and, 77–83; and leadership in organizations, 10, 149–50; management frames and, 57; race and class consciousness frames, 92–110; social movement organizations and, 7–8; stereotype of welfare and, 80; traditional colorblindness and, 47, 50–52. *See also* African American women; Asian American women; Latinas; Native Americans

women of color organizations, 57–58, 170n25

women's movement, 9, 10–11, 166n1. *See also* NOW

work: ethic of, 27; as liberating force, 22; meaning of, 9, 19; rhetoric of, 22; sexual division of, 22; views of, 32–33, 167n15; welfare parents and, 35

About the Author

ROSE ERNST is Assistant Professor of Political Science and Women Studies at Seattle University.

www.ingramcontent.com/pod-product-compliance
Lightning Source LLC
Chambersburg PA
CBHW060040030426
42334CB00019B/2413